The Ultimate Fuel Tax Refund Guide

Fuel Tax Refunds Made Easy

By Justin Dougherty

The Ultimate Fuel Tax Refund Guide.

ISBN: 978-0-9882981-0-1 (Paperback edition)

ISBN: 978-0-9882981-1-8 (Digital edition)

This Book Does Not Provide Financial Advice

The contents of *The Ultimate Fuel Tax Refund Guide* ("Book"), such as text, graphics, images, information obtained from other sources, and other material contained in the Book ("Content") are for informational purposes only. The Content is not intended to be a substitute for professional, financial advice. Never disregard professional advice or delay in seeking it because of something read in this Book.

Use of Content

The Content is protected by copyright under both United States and foreign laws. Title to the Content remains with Justin Dougherty ("Author") or his heirs, assigns and/or licensors. Any copying and/or distribution of the Content not expressly permitted by law may violate copyright, trademark, and other laws and may subject one to damages of up to $150,000 per infringement.

Liability of Author

The use of the Book and the Content is at your own risk.

The Book and Content are provided on an "as is" basis. THE AUTHOR, HIS HEIRS, ASSIGNS AND/OR LICENSORS, TO THE FULLEST EXTENT PERMITTED BY LAW, DISCLAIM ALL WARRANTIES, EITHER EXPRESS OR IMPLIED, STATUTORY OR OTHERWISE, INCLUDING BUT NOT LIMITED TO THE IMPLIED WARRANTIES OF MERCHANTABILITY, NON-INFRINGEMENT OF THIRD PARTIES' RIGHTS, AND FITNESS FOR PARTICULAR PURPOSE. Without limiting the foregoing, the Author, his heirs, assigns and/or licensors make no representations or warranties about the accuracy, reliability, completeness, or timeliness of the Content provided in or through the use of the Book.

In no event shall the Author, his heirs, assigns and/or licensors, or any third parties mentioned in the Book be liable for any damages (including, without limitation, incidental and consequential damages, personal injury/wrongful death, lost profits, or damages resulting from lost data or business interruption) resulting from the use of or inability to use the Book or the Content in attempts to obtain a fuel tax refund or for any other purpose, whether based on warranty, contract, tort, or any other legal theory, and whether or not the Author, his heirs, assigns and/or licensors, or any third parties mentioned in the Book are advised of the possibility of such damages. The Author, his heirs, assigns and/or licensors, or any third parties mentioned in the Book are not liable for any personal injury, including death, caused by your use or misuse of the Book or Content.

Table of Contents

Introduction

The purpose of *The Ultimate Fuel Tax Refund Guide* is for individuals and businesses to save money on the high price of fuel. Both Federal and state governments allow businesses and individuals to file a refund or claim credit on the state and Federal motor fuel excise taxes added to the selling price of fuel. Most of these refund claims require that the applicant submit copies of the original invoices or receipts indicating that fuel taxes were paid on a fuel purchase along with documentation that proves that the fuel was placed into a type of equipment or vehicle. Within the pages of this book one may discover that many exemptions and refunds are common such as for fuel purchased for farming equipment, while others are not widely published as is the case with refunds for fuel purchased for ATVs and on-highway vehicles. Most of the information in this guide comes from an exhaustive review of state and Federal statutes, government forms, conversations with auditors, and direct experience. When put to use, the information in this guide may save individuals, small businesses, corporations and various organizations millions of dollars in taxes paid on fuel.

The high price of fuel.

Most studies of fuel prices clearly show that taxes account for 11 to 12% of the total price of fuel (starting on pg. 10 is a listing of all fuel taxes and fees in the United States).

Figure A: What goes into the price of gasoline in the United States.

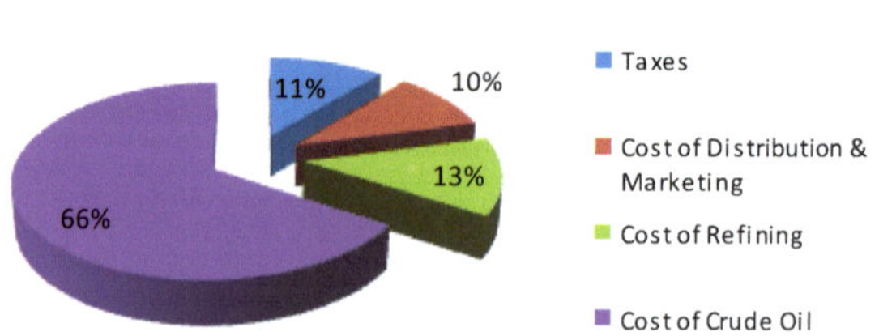

Source: U.S. Energy Information Administration
Note: Based on the average price of gasoline in May 2012 ($3.73/gal).

The Federal and state taxing authorities distribute these taxes for the maintenance of roads and highways. These fuel taxes, along with the high price of fuel, cause many individuals and businesses to search for ways to give them more spending power with their fuel purchases. Often, the cost of fuel can be a heavy burden on budgets and one may choose extreme routes to reduce fuel costs. Taking advantage of the various refund opportunities available in this guide presents a practical and legal means of retrieving the money paid on fuel taxes. Even though many refund opportunities exist for fuel taxes, state governments usually do not actively promote these opportunities to individuals and businesses.

Figure B: What goes into the price of diesel in the United States.

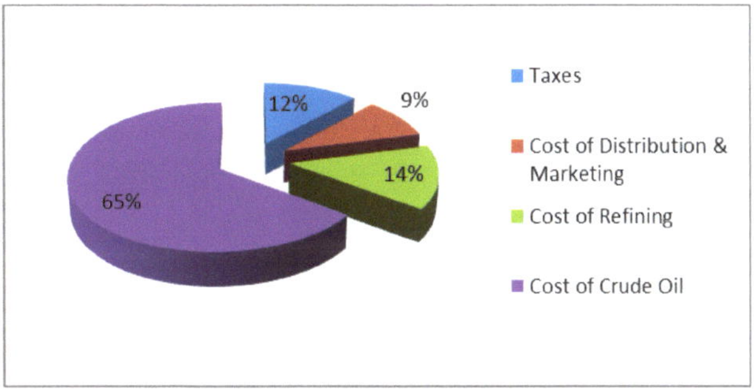

Source: U.S. Energy Information Administration
Note: Based on the average price of diesel in May 2012 ($3.93/gal).

Compounding this issue further, even when these reimbursement allowances are disclosed to the public, oftentimes the filing system can be difficult to understand and confusing. This guide assists the reader by providing a comprehensive state-by-state presentation on all requirements for obtaining certain refunds on the taxes paid on fuel. As of this writing, *The Ultimate Fuel Tax Refund Guide* is the most comprehensive book released on this topic.

The Fuel Tax Refund Process

Most states have similar requirements for submitting a fuel tax refund. For example, some states require original invoices and receipts of the purchased fuel when submitting a refund claim while others accept copies. Since all refund claims are subject to an examination by audit, it is recommended that the following be observed when submitting an initial refund request. The following process must be utilized to maximize one's efforts in securing a fuel tax refund.

- **Create an equipment list**. Upon filing the first refund application for review, the state or Federal government will more than likely require a complete list of any and all equipment fueled. Most state governments require the applicant to submit a list of owned and leased vehicles and equipment. The equipment can be owned or leased just as long as it can be verified through fuel logs or receipts that the equipment was in one's possession when it was fueled. A good way to provide this information is by keeping an up-to-date spreadsheet or database with the following information for each vehicle or piece of equipment:

Suggested Fields for Equipment List

Type of equipment. This could be a car, truck, tractor, trailer or even a plane.

Unit number. The unit number is often used as a shortened form of the equipment's unique identifier. For example, the unit number for a truck in a fleet could be the last five or six numbers of a vehicle's VIN # to easily identify it.

VIN or ID number. The VIN or ID number is often required to confirm the validity of a vehicle.

Make. The vehicle's brand or manufacturer.

Model. The vehicle's model.

Year. The vehicle's year.

Gross Vehicle Weight (GVW). The equipment or vehicle's gross vehicle weight.

Unladen Weight (ULW). The equipment or vehicle's unladen weight.

Ownership status. If the equipment is owned or leased.

IRP number. If the vehicle does not cross state lines and is below a weight threshold then it will not require an IRP account number. IRP information usually appears on the vehicle's registration if the vehicle is registered under an IRP account. If this information does not appear on the vehicle's registration then more than likely the vehicle travels in- state exclusively.

Fleet ID. Only for IRP permitted vehicles. The Fleet ID often appears next to the IRP number on the vehicle's cab card.

Type of fuel. Gasoline, diesel, biodiesel, etc...

State. The state where the vehicle or equipment is licensed.

Vehicle purpose. What the vehicle does plays a pivotal role in the fuel tax refund process. (i.e. waste collection service, construction, taxicab service, etc.)

Status. Depending on the scope of one's inventory, it is a good practice to keep track of in and out-of-service dates. The author of this book recommends writing a short note indicating that the vehicle is active or disposed. (i.e. "Active since Jan 1, 2010, was out of service from Jan-Mar 2005")

Date of first use. This is the date the equipment or vehicle was first used.

IFTA account number. If the applicant owns an IFTA qualified vehicle (26,000 lbs. GVW or above) and the vehicle travels out-of-state then the applicant must pay IFTA taxes. Many companies that file claims also pay IFTA taxes and the taxing authority will sometimes ask for the IFTA account number for the IFTA return.

Number of axles. Number of axles the vehicle or equipment has.

Original leased cost. The leased value of the equipment may be required.

Original purchased price. If the equipment or vehicle has been purchased, the original purchase value may be required.

Auxiliary component. Many vehicles are considered PTO (power take-off). These vehicles include an auxiliary component that is powered from a separate fuel tank. In most states, the fuel that powers these components allows the user to file a fuel tax refund.

- **Create a fuel log of your fuel purchases.** Most fuel purchases for vehicles are recorded in three ways: bulk storage invoices, fuel receipts, and cardlock invoices.

a.) ***Bulk storage invoices***. When fuel is ordered in bulk from a fuel supplier, the fuel is sent by transport to the delivery location AST (above ground storage tank) or UST (underground storage tank). The invoice typically shows the total gallons placed in the tank along with any associated fees or taxes.

b.) ***Fuel receipts***. When fuel is purchased for a single vehicle at a gas station, the state's excise taxes are listed somewhere on the receipt. Federal motor fuel taxes are typically added even though they may not be separately stated. If the fuel is purchased by an employee of a company then these receipts are collected for an expense report, and the cost of the fuel is remitted back to the employee's personal account.

c.) ***Cardlock invoices.*** Cardlock invoices record fuel purchases for an entire fleet. Oftentimes, drivers are provided with a card that allows for the purchase of fuel at a gas station without them paying for the cost of fuel out of pocket. The fuel supplier, in turn, provides an itemized listing of fuel purchases to the purchaser.

Cardlock invoices can often be a substitute for providing fuel logs; however, when cardlock invoices are not available, fuel logs can be used as a means of recording fuel purchases. Below is an example of a fuel log.

Figure C: Example of fuel log.

Fuel Purchases in Gallons - January 2012				
Vehicle Unit #	**Jan 1st**	**Jan 2nd**	**Jan 3rd**	**Jan 4th**
C123	10			
C124	43			45
C125			45	
C126		34		
C127	12			56

The fuel logs ultimately are the best way to consolidate may different fuel purchases in a single spreadsheet. Furthermore, they speed up the refund process by allowing auditors less time to authenticate many different fuel purchases upon their review.

- **Complete the refund claim.** *The Ultimate Fuel Tax Refund Guide* provides a list of every single fuel tax refund claim available to individuals and businesses. Fuel tax refunds come in two forms: return-based and refund-based. Return-based refunds are filed to receive a tax credit that can be taken on a tax return. Licensed fuel suppliers and distributors generally claim a return-based refund credit on their monthly fuel tax returns. Fuel purchasers file refund-based claims in order to obtain a refund from the state or Federal government. Please adhere to the following for filing either a refund or a return based claim.

a.) ***Review the refund or return instructions***. The refund claim instructions contained in this book are there for the reader to determine if a refund or credit opportunity is available for any fuel purchased. The refund instructions provide an easy-to-read way of understanding a refund application or credit without reading through pages of forms and state laws. For example, if a business purchases undyed diesel fuel within the state of Arizona for construction equipment, on pg. 55 is a refund summary giving instructions on how to file that refund claim.

b.) ***Review the state and Federal tax rates***. Starting on pg. 13 is a list of fuel tax rates charged by each state for the purchase or gasoline and diesel fuel. Each rate provides the reader with a means of determining how much the filer can obtain from the taxing authority. For example, if 1,000 gallons of undyed diesel fuel is purchased and used within the State of Pennsylvania for which a refund is available, the filer may file a refund for 38.1 cents per gallon with the state government (i.e. .381 x 1,000 = $380.00). Likewise, for that same fuel, the filer may also file a Federal refund claim (i.e. .244 x 1,000 = $244.00).

c.) ***Review statute of limitations.*** On pg. 45 is a list of all statute of limitations for each state. This list gives the reader an idea of how far back the filer can obtain a refund claim if the filer purchases fuel in various locations.

d.) ***Download or request the refund claim(s).*** For each refund claim listed is a web link to the form(s) required to file a claim. Some claims are not available on-line and do require a request via phone or writing to the state taxing authority.

e.) ***File both state and Federal claims with supporting documents.*** Each refund summary has a section identifying what supporting documentation is required for each fuel tax refund claim to be accepted. Include a copy of the equipment list and fuel log summary (discussed on pgs. 8-9) with your claim if the form calls for it. Make copies of all supporting documents in the event the state fuel tax auditor issues a request for additional documentation.

All Gasoline Fuel Taxes

ALABAMA	
Highway Gasoline Taxes	Cents Per Gallon
State Excise Tax	0.16
Federal Excise Tax	0.184
Underground Storage Tax	0.0125
Total:	0.357

ALASKA	
Highway Gasoline Taxes	Cents Per Gallon
State Excise Tax	0.08
Federal Excise Tax	0.184
Total:	0.264

ARKANSAS	
Highway Gasoline Taxes	Cents Per Gallon
State Excise Tax	0.215
Federal Excise Tax	0.184
Petroleum Environmental Fee	0.003
Total:	0.402

ARIZONA	
Highway Gasoline Taxes	Cents Per Gallon
State Excise Tax	0.18
Federal Excise Tax	0.184
Underground Storage Tax	0.01
Total:	0.374

CALIFORNIA	
Highway Gasoline Taxes	Cents Per Gallon
Combined State, Local, and County Sales Tax Rate	0.2906
Average State District Sales Tax	0.0139
State Excise Tax	0.357
Federal Excise Tax	0.184
Underground Storage Tax	0.02
Total:	0.866

COLORADO	
Highway Gasoline Taxes	Cents Per Gallon
State Excise Tax	0.22
Federal Excise Tax	0.184
Total:	0.404

CONNECTICUT	
Highway Gasoline Taxes	Cents Per Gallon
Sales Tax (6.35% on 7/1/11)	0.202
State Excise Tax (as of 12/31/11)	0.25
Federal Excise Tax	0.184
Total:	0.636

DELAWARE	
Highway Gasoline Taxes	Cents Per Gallon
State Excise Tax	0.23
Federal Excise Tax	0.184
Total:	0.414

D.C., WASHINGTON	
Highway Gasoline Taxes	Cents Per Gallon
State Excise Tax	0.235
Federal Excise Tax	0.184
Total:	0.419

FLORIDA	
Highway Gasoline Taxes	Cents Per Gallon
Sales Tax	0.126
State Excise Tax (As of 1/1/12)	0.166
Constitutional Fuel Tax	0.02
County Fuel Tax	0.01
Municipal Fuel Tax	0.01
Ninth-cent Fuel Tax Avg (0 - 0.010)	0.008
Local Option Fuel Tax	0.060
Additional Local Option Fuel Tax Average (0 -.050)	0.019
Federal Excise Tax	0.184
State Comprehensive Enhanced Transportation System (SCETS) tax, based on the National Consumer Price Index	0.069
Total:	0.672

GEORGIA	
Highway Gasoline Taxes	Cents Per Gallon
State Sales Tax (Depends on county sales takes place in)	0.0956
State Excise Tax	0.075
Federal Excise Tax	0.184
Total:	0.355

HAWAII	
Highway Gasoline Taxes	Cents Per Gallon
Gross Receipts Tax (4%). This rate may vary based on which county the sale takes place.	0.127
State Excise Tax	0.17
County Excise Tax	0 - 0.025
Federal Excise Tax	0.184
Environmental Response Tax. The environmental response tax is 5 cents per barrel (42 U. S. gallons) of petroleum product sold by a distributor to any retail dealer or end user (other than a refiner) of the petroleum product.	0.01
Total:	0.491 to 0.516

IDAHO	
Highway Gasoline Taxes	Cents Per Gallon
State Excise Tax	0.25
Federal Excise Tax	0.184
Total:	0.434

ILLINOIS	
Highway Gasoline Taxes	Cents Per Gallon
State Sales Tax	0.1991
DuPage, Kane, or McHenry County. County Motor Fuel Tax	0.04
State Excise Tax	0.19
Federal Excise Tax	0.184
Environmental Impact Fee	0.008
Underground Storage Fee	0.003
Total:	0.624

INDIANA	
Highway Gasoline Taxes	Cents Per Gallon
State Sales Tax	0.223
State Excise Tax	0.18
Federal Excise Tax	0.184
Oil Inspection Fee	0.01
Total:	0.597

IOWA	
Highway Gasoline Taxes	Cents Per Gallon
State Excise Tax	0.21
Federal Excise Tax	0.184
Underground Storage Tank (UST) Fee	0.01
Total:	0.404

KANSAS	
Highway Gasoline Taxes	Cents Per Gallon
State Excise Tax	0.24
Federal Excise Tax	0.184
Environmental Assurance Fee	0.01
Total:	0.434

KENTUCKY	
Highway Gasoline Taxes	Cents Per Gallon
State Excise Tax	0.264
Federal Excise Tax	0.184
Total:	0.448

LOUISIANA	
Highway Gasoline Taxes	Cents Per Gallon
State Excise Tax	0.20
Federal Excise Tax	0.184
Total:	0.384

MAINE	
Highway Gasoline Taxes	Cents Per Gallon
State Excise Tax Effective 07/01/11	0.30
Federal Excise Tax	0.184
Total:	0.484

MARYLAND	
Highway Gasoline Taxes	Cents Per Gallon
State Excise Tax	0.235
Federal Excise Tax	0.184
Total:	0.419

MASSACHUSETTS	
Highway Gasoline Taxes	Cents Per Gallon
State Excise Tax	0.21
Federal Excise Tax	0.184
Underground Storage Fee	0.025
Total:	0.419

MICHIGAN	
Highway Gasoline Taxes	Cents Per Gallon
State Sales Tax (6%)	0.1722
State Excise Tax	0.19
Federal Excise Tax	0.184
Michigan Underground Storage Tank Financial Assurance Fund (MUSTFA) fee	0.0875
Total:	0.634

MINNESOTA	
Highway Gasoline Taxes	Cents Per Gallon
State Excise Tax	0.28
Federal Excise Tax	0.184
June 1 through Sept. 30, 2011	0.02
Inspection fee (as of 7/1/04)	0.001
Total:	0.485

MISSOURI	
Highway Gasoline Taxes	Cents Per Gallon
State Excise Tax	0.17
Federal Excise Tax	0.184
Agriculture Inspection Fee	0.0005
Transport Load Fee	0.0025
Total:	0.357

MISSISSIPPI	
Highway Gasoline Taxes	Cents Per Gallon
State Excise Tax	0.18
Federal Excise Tax	0.184
Environmental Protection Fee	0.004
Hancock, Harrison and Jackson County "Seawall" Tax	0.03
Total:	0.398

MONTANA	
Highway Gasoline Taxes	Cents Per Gallon
State Excise Tax	0.27
Federal Excise Tax	0.184
Cleanup Fee	0.0075
Total:	0.462

NEVADA	
Highway Gasoline Taxes	Cents Per Gallon
State Excise Tax	.2646 – .3136
Federal Excise Tax	0.184
Total:	.449 to .498

NEW HAMPSHIRE	
Highway Gasoline Taxes	Cents Per Gallon
State Excise Tax	0.18
Federal Excise Tax	0.184
Total:	0.364

NEW JERSEY	
Highway Gasoline Taxes	Cents Per Gallon
State Excise Tax	0.105
Federal Excise Tax	0.184
Petroleum Products Gross Receipts Tax	0.04
Total:	0.329

NEW MEXICO	
Highway Gasoline Taxes	Cents Per Gallon
State Excise Tax	0.17
Federal Excise Tax	0.184
Petroleum products loading fee (PPLF)	0.01875
Total:	0.373

NEW YORK	
Highway Gasoline Taxes	Cents Per Gallon
Sales Tax (Avg rate of 8%)	0.255
State Excise and Supplemental Tax	0.178
Federal Excise Tax	0.184
Total:	0.617

NORTH CAROLINA	
Highway Gasoline Taxes	Cents Per Gallon
State Excise Tax 01/01/12 – 06/30/12	0.389
Federal Excise Tax	0.184
Inspection Fee	0.025
Total:	0.598

NORTH DAKOTA	
Highway Gasoline Taxes	Cents Per Gallon
State Excise Tax	0.23
Federal Excise Tax	0.184
Total:	0.414

OHIO	
Highway Gasoline Taxes	Cents Per Gallon
State Excise Tax	0.28
Federal Excise Tax	0.184
Total:	0.464

OKLAHOMA	
Highway Gasoline Taxes	Cents Per Gallon
State Excise Tax	0.16
Federal Excise Tax	0.184
Underground Storage Fee	0.01
Total:	0.354

OREGON	
Highway Gasoline Taxes	**Cents Per Gallon**
State Excise Tax	0.30
County Excise Tax (Multnomah and Washington County)	0 to .03
City Excise Tax Rate (Various Counties)	0 to .05
Federal Excise Tax	0.184
Total:	.484 to .564

PENNSYLVANIA	
Highway Gasoline Taxes	**Cents Per Gallon**
State Excise Tax	0.312
Federal Excise Tax	0.184
Total:	0.496

RHODE ISLAND	
Highway Gasoline Taxes	**Cents Per Gallon**
State Excise Tax	0.30
Federal Excise Tax	0.184
Uniform oil spill response and prevention fee	0.05
Total:	0.534

SOUTH CAROLINA	
Highway Gasoline Taxes	Cents Per Gallon
State Excise Tax	0.16
Federal Excise Tax	0.184
Inspection Fee	0.0025
Environmental Impact Fee	0.005
Total:	0.351

SOUTH DAKOTA	
Highway Gasoline Taxes	Cents Per Gallon
State Excise Tax	0.22
Federal Excise Tax	0.184
Tank Inspection Fee	0.02
Total:	0.424

TENNESSEE	
Highway Gasoline Taxes	Cents Per Gallon
State Excise Tax	0.20
Federal Excise Tax	0.184
Special Petroleum Fee	0.014
Total:	0.398

TEXAS	
Highway Gasoline Taxes	Cents Per Gallon
State Excise Tax	0.20
Federal Excise Tax	0.184
Total:	0.384

UTAH	
Highway Gasoline Taxes	Cents Per Gallon
State Excise Tax	0.245
Federal Excise Tax	0.184
Total:	0.429

VERMONT	
Highway Gasoline Taxes	Cents Per Gallon
Net use (sales) tax. 2% of the average quarterly retail price.	0.0716
State Excise Tax	0.20
Federal Excise Tax	0.184
Motor Fuel Transportation Infrastructure Assessment (MFTIA) fee. Q2 2012	0.065
Total:	0.521

VIRGINIA	
Highway Gasoline Taxes	Cents Per Gallon
Northern Virginia Transportation District 2.1% Sales Tax	0.067
State Excise Tax	0.175
Federal Excise Tax	0.184
Virginia Tank Storage Fee	0.006
Total:	0.365

WASHINGTON	
Highway Gasoline Taxes	Cents Per Gallon
Net use (sales) tax	0.27
State Excise Tax	0.375
Federal Excise Tax	0.184
Coastal Protection Fund fee	0.01
Total:	0.839

WEST VIRGINIA	
Highway Gasoline Taxes	Cents Per Gallon
Net use (sales) tax. 5% provided the average wholesale price is no less than $2.34 per invoiced gallon.	0.1593
State Excise Tax	0.205
Federal Excise Tax	0.184
Coastal Protection Fund fee	0.01
Total:	0.558

WISCONSIN	
Highway Gasoline Taxes	Cents Per Gallon
State Excise Tax	0.309
Federal Excise Tax	0.184
Total:	0.493

WYOMING	
Highway Gasoline Taxes	Cents Per Gallon
State Excise Tax	0.14
Federal Excise Tax	0.184
Total:	0.324

All Diesel Fuel Taxes

ALABAMA	
Highway Diesel Taxes	Cents Per Gallon
State Excise Tax	0.19
Federal Excise Tax	0.244
Underground Storage Tax	0.0125
Total:	0.447

ALASKA	
Highway Diesel Taxes	Cents Per Gallon
State Excise Tax	0.08
Federal Excise Tax	0.244
Total:	0.324

ARKANSAS	
Highway Diesel Taxes	Cents Per Gallon
State Excise Tax	0.225
Federal Excise Tax	0.244
Petroleum Environmental Fee	0.003
Total:	0.472

ARIZONA	
Highway Diesel Taxes	Cents Per Gallon
State Excise Tax	0.18
Federal Excise Tax	0.244
Underground Storage Tax	0.01
Total:	0.434

CALIFORNIA	
Highway Diesel Taxes	Cents Per Gallon
Combined State, Local, and County Sales Tax Rate	0.317
Average State District Sales Tax	0.0139
State Excise Tax	0.13
Federal Excise Tax	0.244
Underground Storage Tax	0.02
Total:	0.725

COLORADO	
Highway Diesel Taxes	Cents Per Gallon
State Excise Tax	0.205
Federal Excise Tax	0.244
Total:	0.449

CONNECTICUT	
Highway Diesel Taxes	Cents Per Gallon
Sales Tax (6.35% on 7/1/11)	0.221
State Excise Tax (as of 12/31/11)	0.462
Federal Excise Tax	0.244
Total:	0.927

DELAWARE	
Highway Diesel Taxes	Cents Per Gallon
State Excise Tax	0.22
Federal Excise Tax	0.244
Total:	0.464

D.C., WASHINGTON	
Highway Diesel Taxes	Cents Per Gallon
State Excise Tax	0.235
Federal Excise Tax	0.244
Total:	0.479

FLORIDA	
Highway Diesel Taxes	Cents Per Gallon
Sales Tax	0.126
State Excise Tax (As of 1/1/12)	0.305
Constitutional Fuel Tax	0.02
County Fuel Tax	0.01
Municipal Fuel Tax	0.01
Ninth-cent Fuel Tax Avg (0 - 0.010)	0.008
Local Option Fuel Tax	0.06
Additional Local Option Fuel Tax Average (0 -.050)	0.019
Federal Excise Tax	0.244
State Comprehensive Enhanced Transportation System (SCETS) tax, based on the National Consumer Price Index	0.069
Total:	0.871

GEORGIA	
Highway Diesel Taxes	**Cents Per Gallon**
State Sales Tax (Depends on county sales takes place in)	0.1043
State Excise Tax	0.075
Federal Excise Tax	0.244
Total:	0.423

HAWAII	
Highway Diesel Taxes	**Cents Per Gallon**
Gross Receipts Tax (4%). This rate may vary based on which county the sale takes place.	0.139
State Excise Tax	0.17
County Excise Tax	0 - 0.025
Federal Excise Tax	0.244
Environmental Response Tax The environmental response tax is 5 cents per barrel (42 U. S. gallons) of petroleum product sold by a distributor to any retail dealer or end user (other than a refiner) of the petroleum product.	0.01
Total:	0.563 to 0.588

IDAHO	
Highway Diesel Taxes	**Cents Per Gallon**
State Excise Tax	0.25
Federal Excise Tax	0.244
Total:	0.494

ILLINOIS	
Highway Diesel Taxes	Cents Per Gallon
State Sales Tax	0.2173
DuPage, Kane, or McHenry County. County Motor Fuel Tax	0.04
State Excise Tax	0.215
Federal Excise Tax	0.244
Environmental Impact Fee	0.008
Underground Storage Fee	0.003
Total:	0.727

INDIANA	
Highway Diesel Taxes	Cents Per Gallon
State Sales Tax	0.2433
State Excise Tax	0.16
Federal Excise Tax	0.244
Oil Inspection Fee	0.01
Total:	0.657

IOWA	
Highway Diesel Taxes	Cents Per Gallon
State Excise Tax	0.225
Federal Excise Tax	0.244
Underground Storage Tank (UST) Fee	0.01
Total:	0.479

KANSAS	
Highway Diesel Taxes	Cents Per Gallon
State Excise Tax	0.26
Federal Excise Tax	0.244
Environmental Assurance Fee	0.01
Total:	0.514

KENTUCKY	
Highway Diesel Taxes	Cents Per Gallon
State Excise Tax	0.234
Federal Excise Tax	0.244
Total:	0.478

LOUISIANA	
Highway Diesel Taxes	Cents Per Gallon
State Excise Tax	0.20
Federal Excise Tax	0.244
Total:	0.444

MAINE	
Highway Diesel Taxes	Cents Per Gallon
State Excise Tax	0.312
Federal Excise Tax	0.244
	0.556

MARYLAND	
Highway Diesel Taxes	Cents Per Gallon
State Excise Tax	0.2425
Federal Excise Tax	0.244
Total:	0.487

MASSACHUSETTS	
Highway Diesel Taxes	Cents Per Gallon
State Excise Tax	0.21
Federal Excise Tax	0.244
Underground Storage Fee	0.025
Total:	0.479

MICHIGAN	
Highway Diesel Taxes	Cents Per Gallon
State Sales Tax (6%)	0.1722
State Excise Tax	0.1500
Federal Excise Tax	0.244
Michigan Underground Storage Tank Financial Assurance Fund (MUSTFA) fee	0.0875
	0.6537

MINNESOTA	
Highway Diesel Taxes	Cents Per Gallon
State Excise Tax	0.28
Federal Excise Tax	0.244
Clean-up fee effective June 1 through Sept. 30, 2011	0.02
Inspection fee	0.001
Total:	0.545

MISSOURI	
Highway Diesel Taxes	Cents Per Gallon
State Excise Tax	0.17
Federal Excise Tax	0.244
Agriculture Inspection Fee	0.0005
Transport Load Fee	0.0025
Total:	0.417

MISSISSIPPI	
Highway Diesel Taxes	Cents Per Gallon
State Excise Tax	0.18
Federal Excise Tax	0.244
Environmental Protection Fee	0.004
Hancock, Harrison and Jackson County "Seawall" Tax	0.03
Total:	0.458

MONTANA	
Highway Diesel Taxes	Cents Per Gallon
State Excise Tax	0.2775
Federal Excise Tax	0.244
Cleanup Fee	0.0075
Total:	0.529

NEVADA	
Highway Diesel Taxes	Cents Per Gallon
State Excise Tax	0.265
Federal Excise Tax	0.244
	0.509

NEW HAMPSHIRE	
Highway Diesel Taxes	Cents Per Gallon
State Excise Tax	0.18
Federal Excise Tax	0.244
Total:	0.424

NEW JERSEY	
Highway Diesel Taxes	Cents Per Gallon
State Excise Tax	0.135
Federal Excise Tax	0.244
Petroleum Products Gross Receipts Tax	0.04
Total:	0.419

NEW MEXICO	
Highway Diesel Taxes	Cents Per Gallon
State Excise Tax	0.21
Federal Excise Tax	0.244
Petroleum products loading fee (PPLF)	0.01875
Total:	0.473

NEW YORK	
Highway Diesel Taxes	Cents Per Gallon
Sales Tax (avg rate of 8%)	0.278
State Excise and Supplemental Tax	0.161
Federal Excise Tax	0.244
Total:	0.683

NORTH CAROLINA	
Highway Diesel Taxes	Cents Per Gallon
State Excise Tax 01/01/12 – 06/30/12	0.389
Federal Excise Tax	0.244
Inspection Fee	0.025
Total:	0.658

NORTH DAKOTA	
Highway Diesel Taxes	Cents Per Gallon
State Excise Tax	0.230
Federal Excise Tax	0.244
Total:	0.474

OHIO	
Highway Diesel Taxes	Cents Per Gallon
State Excise Tax	0.28
Federal Excise Tax	0.244
Total:	0.524

OKLAHOMA	
Highway Diesel Taxes	Cents Per Gallon
State Excise Tax	0.13
Federal Excise Tax	0.244
Underground Storage Fee	0.01
Total:	0.384

OREGON	
Highway Diesel Taxes	Cents Per Gallon
State Excise Tax	0.30
County Excise Tax	0
City Excise Tax Rate	0 to .05
Federal Excise Tax	0.244
Total:	.544 to .594

PENNSYLVANIA	
Highway Diesel Taxes	Cents Per Gallon
State Excise Tax	0.381
Federal Excise Tax	0.244
Total:	0.625

RHODE ISLAND	
Highway Diesel Taxes	Cents Per Gallon
State Excise Tax	0.30
Federal Excise Tax	0.244
Uniform oil spill response and prevention fee	0.05
Total:	0.594

SOUTH CAROLINA	
Highway Diesel Taxes	Cents Per Gallon
State Excise Tax	0.16
Federal Excise Tax	0.244
Inspection Fee	0.0025
Environmental Impact Fee	0.005
Total:	0.412

SOUTH DAKOTA	
Highway Diesel Taxes	Cents Per Gallon
State Excise Tax	0.22
Federal Excise Tax	0.244
Tank Inspection Fee	0.02
Total:	0.484

TENNESSEE	
Highway Diesel Taxes	Cents Per Gallon
State Excise Tax	0.17
Federal Excise Tax	0.244
Special Petroleum Fee	0.014
Total:	0.428

TEXAS	
Highway Diesel Taxes	Cents Per Gallon
State Excise Tax	0.200
Federal Excise Tax	0.244
Total:	0.444

UTAH	
Highway Diesel Taxes	**Cents Per Gallon**
State Excise Tax	0.245
Federal Excise Tax	0.244
Total:	0.489

VERMONT	
Highway Diesel Taxes	**Cents Per Gallon**
Net use (sales) tax. 2% of the average quarterly retail price.	0.079
State Excise Tax	0.29
Federal Excise Tax	0.244
Motor Fuel Transportation Infrastructure Assessment (MFTIA) fee. Q2 2012	0.03
Total:	0.643

VIRGINIA	
Highway Diesel Taxes	**Cents Per Gallon**
Northern Virginia Transportation District 2.1% Sales Tax	0.073
State Excise Tax	0.175
Federal Excise Tax	0.244
Virginia Tank Storage Fee	0.006
Total:	0.425

WASHINGTON	
Highway Diesel Taxes	Cents Per Gallon
Net use (sales) tax	0.270
State Excise Tax	0.375
Federal Excise Tax	0.244
Underground Storage Tax	0
Total:	0.889

WEST VIRGINIA	
Highway Diesel Taxes	Cents Per Gallon
Net use (sales) tax. 5% provided the average wholesale price is no less than $2.34 per invoiced gallon.	0.1738
State Excise Tax	0.205
Federal Excise Tax	0.244
Coastal Protection Fund fee	0
Total:	0.623

WISCONSIN	
Highway Diesel Taxes	Cents Per Gallon
State Excise Tax	0.309
Federal Excise Tax	0.244
Total:	0.553

WYOMING	
Highway Diesel Taxes	Cents Per Gallon
State Excise Tax	0.14
Federal Excise Tax	0.244
Total:	0.384

Frequently Asked Questions

1.) ***Is fuel subject to sales tax?*** Yes, in some states it is. For example, in Iowa gasoline and diesel fuel are exempt from sales tax when used on the highway or in watercraft or aircraft if the fuel tax has been paid and no refund of the fuel tax has been allowed. When a fuel tax refund is allowed, the sales tax is deducted from the refund unless it is used for a function that is exempt from sales tax. In some instances, the amount of sales tax which would be due may exceed the amount of fuel tax refund allowed. This can happen because the fuel tax rate is a fixed amount per gallon and is not impacted by the price of fuel. On the other hand, sales tax is based on the price paid for the fuel, so as the price goes up, the sales tax also goes up. If this situation occurs, taxpayers may elect to not claim the fuel tax refund, since if they did, they would owe the difference between the sales tax and the fuel tax refund. *The Ultimate Fuel Tax Refund Guide* has taken great pains to indicate which states charge tax on a particular fuel tax refund. For each refund listed the refund summary will indicate if sales tax is due or not.

2.) ***Is sales tax due when a refund is received? If so, how does one know if sales tax is due on a refund or not?*** It depends. Each refund summary in this book identifies if sales tax is required or not. In most instances this tax is deducted from the total refund. Since it does not make sense to file a refund claim if the tax is greater than the refund itself, the author of this book has identified any claims where this is the case. It is recommended that the claimant calculate the refund before filing the claim. Below are two scenarios where a claimant may pay sales tax on a claim.

Example A: 10,000 gallons of diesel fuel purchased at $1.50 per gallon.
Purchase Price: 10,000 X $1.50 = $15,000.00.
Fuel Tax Paid: 10,000 gallons X 22.5 cents per gallon = $2,250.00.
Net Cost of Fuel: ($1.50 - $0.225) X 10,000 = $12,750.00.
Sales Tax (6%): $12,750 X 0.06 = $765.00.
Net Refund: $2,250 - $765 = $1,485.00.

File this claim since this scenario produces a net refund.

Example B: 10,000 gallons of diesel fuel purchased at $4.50 per gallon.
Purchase Price: 10,000 X $4.50 = $45,000
Fuel Tax Paid: 10,000 gallons x 22.5 cents per gallon = $2,250
Net Cost of Fuel: ($4.50 - $0.225) X 10,000 = $42,750
Sales Tax (6%): $42,750 X 0.06 = $2,565
Net Refund: $2,250 - $2,565 = [$315]

Do not file this claim since this scenario results in a liability.

3.) ***What are the statutes of limitation per each state?*** See pg. 41 for a listing for each State.

4.) ***When can I expect my refund?*** Most states will issue a refund within 2-4 months.

5.) ***Can I hire a company or accountant to take care of this for me?*** Yes, a business or accountant may be hired to file a refund claim on behalf of an individual, business or other organization. Please be advised that a valid POA-1 (Power of Attorney Form) must be on file with the state taxing authority processing the refund.

6.) ***How much can I expect back?*** This typically depends on three factors: 1) the amount of fuel purchased, 2.) the tax rate of the state the fuel was purchased in and 3.) if sales taxes are due on the refund.

7.) ***Where does the information in this book come from?*** The information contained in this book comes from state statutes, tax forms and conversations with state tax auditors.

8.) ***Can I get a refund on the taxes I pay on the fuel I put in my truck?*** *Yes, only* if the truck uses fuel while idling, operates off-highway, or uses fuel for an auxiliary component on the truck, the Federal government and most states allow a refund for that fuel usage.

9.) ***Can I get a refund on the fuel taxes I pay for my lawn equipment?***
Yes, many states allow a fuel tax exemption for off-road usage and this includes lawn equipment.

10.) ***Will I or my businesses be audited if I file a fuel tax claim?***
The writer of *The Ultimate Fuel Tax Refund Guide* defers to the appropriate taxing authority allowing the refund to make that decision. As a side note, this book advises the claim applicant to retain certain documents in the event of an audit.

11.) ***If I need to contact the fuel tax group of a certain state do you have a list of phone numbers available?***
Starting on pg. 252 is a listing of phone numbers for each government fuel tax section of each state.

12.) How do I know if I paid state fuel taxes on my fuel?

The fuel purchase price usually includes fuel taxes. If motor fuel is sold without excise tax, the receipt should indicate that fuel taxes were not charged. Sales tax is charged at a percentage of the selling price only in certain states. Excise tax is a set amount per gallon.

13.) How come no refunds are listed for Mississippi?

No fuel tax refunds exist for Mississippi.

Statutes of Limitations

State	Statute of Limitations / Filing Date
AL	For most refunds, 3 years from the date the fuel was purchased.
AK	1 year from the date the fuel was purchased.
AZ	For most refunds: Licensed filer - 3 years from the date was purchased. Unlicensed filer - 6 months from the date the fuel purchased.
AR	1 year from the date the fuel was purchased.
CA	3 years from the date the fuel was purchased.
CO	1 year from the date the fuel was purchased.
CT	On or before May 31th, for fuel purchased in the preceding calendar year.
DE	1 year from the date the fuel was purchased.
DC	The 25th day of the month following the month when the fuel was purchased.
FL	For most refunds, 3 years from the date the fuel was purchased.
GA	18 months from the date the fuel was purchased.
HI	For most refunds, the 20th day of the month following the month when the fuel was purchased.
ID	3 years from the date the fuel was purchased.
IL	Unlicensed distributor or supplier: 2 years ago or less. Licensed distributors and suppliers: 1 year ago or less.
IN	For most refunds, 3 years from the date the fuel was purchased.
IA	3 years from the date the fuel was purchased.
KS	1 year from the date the fuel was purchased.
KY	4 years from the date the fuel was purchased.
LA	For most refunds, 6 months from the date the fuel was purchased.
ME	1 year from the date the fuel was purchased.
MI	For most refunds, 18 months from the date the fuel was purchased.
MN	1 year and 2 months (425 days) from the date the fuel was purchased.

State	Statute of Limitations / Filing Date
MS	No refund opportunities.
MA	2 years from the date the fuel was purchased.
MD	1 year from the date the fuel was purchased.
MO	1 year from the date of purchase or April 15 following the year of the purchase. Whichever is later.
MT	For most refunds, 3 years from the date the fuel was purchased.
NC	For most refunds, claims for refund may be filed up to three years from the due date.
ND	Claims for refund are due by June 30th for fuel purchases made for the prior year.
NE	For most refunds, 3 years from the date the fuel was purchased.
NV	1 year from the date the fuel was purchased.
NH	April 15 following the year of purchase for an annual claim.
NJ	6 months from the date the fuel was purchased.
NM	For most refunds, 6 months from the date the fuel was purchased.
NY	For most refunds, 2 years from the date the fuel was purchased.
OH	365 days from the date the fuel was purchased.
OK	3 years following the last day of the calendar month in which the fuel tax was paid.
OR	15 months from the date the fuel was purchased.
PA	For most refunds, filers must submit reimbursement claims (postmarked) on or before the 60th day following the end of each calendar quarter.
RI	240 days from the date the fuel was purchased.
SC	3 years from the date the fuel was purchased.
SD	For most refunds, 3 years from the date the fuel was purchased.
TN	For most refunds: Licensed filer - 3 Years from the date was purchased. Unlicensed filer - 6 months from the date the fuel purchased.
TX	1 year from purchase or use of it withdrawn for own use. 4 years for overpayment.
UT	3 years from the date the fuel was purchased.
VA	1 year from the date on the Invoice showing the fuel purchase.
VT	33 months following the due date of the report covering the reporting period in which the purchase was made.
WA	13 months from the date the fuel was purchased.
WV	For most refunds, 30 days from the month the fuel was purchased.
WI	1 year from the date the fuel was purchased.
WY	1 year from the date the fuel was purchased.

Key for Refund Instructions

FIELD	DEFINITION
State the fuel is purchased in:	*The state or jurisdiction where the fuel was purchased. In all cases a refund claim is filed with that state or jurisdiction's taxing authority.*
Fuel type:	*The type(s) of fuel purchased and taxed.*
Refund type:	*The type(s) of equipment fueled or the qualification for refund.*
Form name:	*The name of the refund claim provided by the state or Federal taxing authority.*
Form #:	*The specific form number of the refund claim.*
Obtain required forms from:	*The web site URL where the refund claim forms can be accessed.*
Tax deducted from refund:	*In some instances, sales tax must be deducted from claim.*
Tax paid on separate return:	*Some claims require the user to deduct taxes on the refund claim itself whereas some states require the filer to remit the tax on a sales and use tax return. For those states that require the filer to pay the tax on a separate return, this is acknowledged under this field for the specific claim.*
Difficulty:	*For each refund claim, the level of simplicity in filling out the refund claim is listed. The level of difficulty depends on such factors as the volume of supporting documentation requested, and how many schedules are required.*
File by:	*Most states require the filer to file the refund claim within a certain period of time based on each state's statute of limitations. For example, if a state's statute of limitation to file a refund claim is 60 days then the filer will need to submit a refund claim within 60 days from the day the fuel was purchased.*
Attach documents to claim:	*Supporting documents requested with refund claim.*
Send to address:	*Address of where to send the claim.*

FIELD	DEFINITION
Don't file if:	*There are certain instances where the filer should not file a refund claim. For instance, there may be dollar threshold amount.*
State statute(s) supporting refund:	*Statute(s) supporting refund claim.*
Keep records on file:	*States require that the individual filing a refund claim keep accurate records in the event of an audit for a certain period of time.*

Federal Fuel Tax Refund Claims

<u>Federal Fuel Tax Refund Claim Instructions</u>: Fuel tax refund for fuel purchased for boats, buses used for mass transit, construction equipment, exports, fabrication equipment, farming equipment, foreign trade, government-owned vehicles, heating, helicopters, idling, logging equipment, manufacturing, mining equipment, non-profit equipment, off-road use, PTO vehicles, reefer trailers, school buses and stationary equipment.

INSTRUCTIONS	
Jurisdiction:	United States
Fuel type:	Aviation gasoline, biodiesel, CNG (compressed natural gas), gasoline, kerosene used in aviation, LPG (liquid petroleum gas), undyed diesel fuel, undyed kerosene and other fuels.
Refund type:	Commercial fishing, construction equipment, exports, fabrication equipment, farming, foreign trade, heating, helicopters, idling, lawn equipment, mining, manufacturing, mass transit buses, non-profit (educational) organizations that own vehicles, off-road use, planes, PTO (power take-off) equipment, refrigeration (reefer) trailers, school buses, state and Federal government agencies, stationary equipment and trains.
Form name:	Various, see below.
Form #:	Note: The taxpayer can file a claim for refund on form 8849 or a credit against fuel tax liability on form 720. The below forms are required for a claim for refund. A fuel tax credit is computed on form 4136, which must be attached to form 1040. Required form(s): **8849**, *Claim for Refund of Excise Taxes.* Additional schedules required based on refund and fuel type: **Schedule 1**, *Nontaxable Use of Fuels.* **Schedule 2**, *Sales by Registered Ultimate Vendors.* **Schedule 3**, *Certain Fuel Mixtures and the Alt. Fuel Credit.* **Schedule 5**, *Section 4081(e) claims.* **Schedule 6**, *Other Claims.* **Schedule 8**, *Registered Credit Card Issuers.*
Obtain required forms from:	http://www.irs.gov/pub/irs-pdf/f8849.pdf

INSTRUCTIONS FOR FEDERAL CLAIM (CONTINUED)	
Tax Deducted from Refund?	No.
Tax Paid on Separate Return?	No.
Difficulty	Moderate.
Statute of Limitations	The annual Form 8849 for fuel used during the taxable year must be filed within the 3 years following the close of the taxable year.
Required Documents	You are not required to provide the information requested on a form that is subject to the *Paperwork Reduction Act* unless the form displays a valid OMB control number. Books or records relating to a form or its instructions must be retained as long as their contents may become material in the administration of any Internal Revenue law.
Send To Address	For Schedules 1 and 6, mail Form 8849 to: Department of the Treasury Internal Revenue Service Cincinnati, OH 45999-0002 For Schedules 2, 3, 5, and 8, mail Form 8849 to: Internal Revenue Service P.O. Box 312 Covington, KY 41012-0312
Don't File If...	N/A.
Federal Law Supporting Refund	26 USC § 6427.
Record Retention	Indefinitely.

STATE FUEL TAX REFUND CLAIMS

ALABAMA

Alabama Fuel Tax Refund Claim Instructions: Fuel tax refund for undyed diesel purchased for boats, construction equipment, farming equipment, logging equipment, mining equipment, off-road use, reefer trailers and stationary equipment.

INSTRUCTIONS	
State the fuel is purchased in:	AL
Fuel type:	Undyed diesel fuel.
Refund type:	Commercial boat use, construction, farming, logging, mining, off-road use, refrigeration (reefer) trailers and stationary equipment.
Form name:	*Claim for Motor Fuel Tax Refund (Off-Road Use).*
Form #:	**SUBT: DR** (Must be notarized).
Obtain required forms from:	http://www.revenue.alabama.gov/motorfuels/mfforms.htm
Tax deducted from refund:	Yes.
Tax paid on separate return:	No.
Difficulty:	Moderate.
File by:	3 years from the date the fuel was purchased.
Attach documents to claim:	Copies of motor fuel receipts or invoices along with an itemized list of fuel purchases or withdraws with the date of fuel withdrawn from the tank / purchased and placed in the vehicle, vehicle type, the equipment ID number and the number of gallons.
Send to address:	Alabama Department of Revenue Sales, Use & Business Tax Division Motor Fuels Section P.O. Box 327540 Montgomery, AL 36132
Don't file if:	Sales tax is greater than refund.
State statute(s) supporting refund:	§ 40-17-2(3), § 40-17-220(g), Code of Alabama 1975.
Keep records on file:	6 Years.

<u>Alabama Fuel Tax Refund Claim Instructions</u>: Fuel tax refund for overpayment of fuel purchased by two petitioners.

INSTRUCTIONS	
State the fuel is purchased in:	AL
Fuel type:	Gasoline, gasohol, jet fuel and undyed diesel fuel.
Refund type:	Overpayment of excise tax by two petitioners.
Form name:	*Joint Petition for Refund.*
Form #:	**SUBT: RJ**.
Obtain required forms from:	http://www.revenue.alabama.gov/motorfuels/mfforms.htm
Tax deducted from refund:	No.
Tax paid on separate return:	No.
Difficulty:	Moderate.
File by:	3 years from the date the fuel was purchased.
Attach documents to claim:	Copies of motor fuel receipts or invoices. The claim must be filed by two or more petitioners where the seller charged, collected and remitted the taxes paid by one or more purchasers.
Send to address:	Alabama Department of Revenue Sales, Use & Business Tax Division Motor Fuels Section P.O. Box 327540 Montgomery, AL 36132
Don't file if:	N/A.
State statute(s) supporting refund:	§ 40-17-2, § 40-17-220, Code of Alabama 1975.
Keep records on file:	6 Years.

<u>Alabama Fuel Tax Refund Claim Instructions</u>: Fuel tax refund for overpayment of fuel purchased by a single petitioner.

INSTRUCTIONS	
State the fuel is purchased in:	AL
Fuel type:	Gasoline, gasohol, jet fuel and undyed diesel fuel.
Refund type:	Overpayment of excise tax by single petitioner, such as a fuel distributor, the Federal and local government, and boards of education.
Form name:	*Petition for Refund.*
Form #:	**SUBT: RP**.
Obtain required forms from:	http://www.revenue.alabama.gov/motorfuels/mfforms.htm
Tax deducted from refund:	No.
Tax paid on separate return:	No.
Difficulty:	Moderate.
File by:	3 years from the date the fuel was purchased.
Attach documents to claim:	Copies of motor fuel receipts or invoices.
Send to address:	Alabama Department of Revenue Sales, Use & Business Tax Division Motor Fuels Section P.O. Box 327540 Montgomery, AL 36132
Don't file if:	N/A.
State statute(s) supporting refund:	§ 40-17-2, § 40-17-220, Code of Alabama 1975.
Keep records on file:	6 Years.

<u>Alabama Fuel Tax Refund Claim Instructions</u>: Fuel tax refund for gasoline purchased and used by charitable organizations, gas districts, volunteer fire departments and water and fire authorities.

INSTRUCTIONS	
State the fuel is purchased in:	AL
Fuel type:	Gasoline.
Refund type:	Charitable organizations, gas districts, volunteer fire departments, water and fire authorities.
Form name:	*Claim for Gasoline Tax Refund.*
Form #:	**SUBT: GR-5**. Note: Must be notarized.
Obtain required forms from:	http://www.revenue.alabama.gov/motorfuels/mfforms.htm
Tax deducted from refund:	No.
Tax paid on separate return:	No.
Difficulty:	Moderate.
File by:	2 years from the date the fuel was purchased.
Attach documents to claim:	Copies of motor fuel receipts or invoices. The receipts or reports must include the date of the purchase, name and address of vendor, product type, invoice number, and number of gallons of fuel purchased. Also required is an itemized list of fuel purchases with the vendor name and address, the date of purchase and the gallons of fuel purchased.
Send to address:	Alabama Department of Revenue Sales, Use & Business Tax Division Motor Fuels Section P.O. Box 327540 Montgomery, AL 36132
Don't file if:	N/A.
State statute(s) supporting refund:	§ 40-9-9, § 40-9-13, § 40-9-23, § 11-22-13, § 11-50-412, § 11-88-16, and § 22-51-13, Code of Alabama 1975.
Keep records on file:	6 Years.

<u>Alabama Fuel Tax Refund Claim Instructions</u>: Fuel tax refund for undyed diesel purchased and used by charitable organizations, gas districts, volunteer fire departments and water and fire authorities.

INSTRUCTIONS	
State the fuel is purchased in:	AL
Fuel type:	Undyed diesel fuel.
Refund type:	Charitable organizations, gas districts, volunteer fire departments, water and fire authorities.
Form name:	*Claim for Motor Fuel Refund.*
Form #:	**SUBT: MF-5**. Note: Must be notarized.
Obtain required forms from:	http://www.revenue.alabama.gov/motorfuels/mfforms.htm
Tax deducted from refund:	No.
Tax paid on separate return:	No.
Difficulty:	Moderate.
File by:	2 years from the date the fuel was purchased.
Attach documents to claim:	Copies of motor fuel receipts or invoices. The receipts or reports must include the date of the purchase, name and address of vendor, product type, invoice number, and number of gallons of fuel purchased. Also required is an itemized list of fuel purchases with the vendor name and address, the date of purchase and the gallons of fuel purchased.
Send to address:	Alabama Department of Revenue Sales, Use & Business Tax Division Motor Fuels Section P.O. Box 327540 Montgomery, AL 36132
Don't file if:	N/A.
State statute(s) supporting refund:	§ 40-9-9, § 40-9-13, § 40-9-23, § 11-22-13, § 11-50-412, § 11-88-16, and § 22-51-13, Code of Alabama 1975.
Keep records on file:	6 Years.

Alabama Fuel Tax Refund Claim Instructions: Fuel tax refund for fuel exports.

INSTRUCTIONS	
State the fuel is purchased in:	AL
Fuel type:	Gasoline, gasohol, jet fuel, lubricating oil and undyed diesel fuel.
Refund type:	Exports.
Form name:	Various, see below.
Form #:	Required form(s): **SUBT: GA-1R**, *Monthly Gasoline Tax Return - Receipts Basis.* **SUBT: GA-1**, *Monthly Gasoline Tax Return - Inventory Basis.* **SUBT: MF-1**, *Monthly Motor Fuel Tax Return - Receipts Basis.* **SUBT: MF-2**, *Monthly Motor Fuel Tax Return – Inventory Basis.* **SUBT: AVFL**, *Monthly Aviation Fuels Tax Return.* **SUBT: LO-1**, *Monthly Lubricating Oils Tax Return.*
Obtain required forms from:	http://www.revenue.alabama.gov/motorfuels/mfforms.htm
Tax deducted from refund:	No.
Tax paid on separate return:	No.
Difficulty:	Difficult.
File by:	Must be filed by the 20th of each month following month of activity.
Attach documents to claim:	Required schedules.
Send to address:	Alabama Department of Revenue Sales, Use & Business Tax Division Motor Fuels Section P.O. Box 327540 Montgomery, AL 36132
Don't file if:	Claimant is not a licensed distributor.
State statute(s) supporting refund:	§ 40-17-329 (a)(1) Code of Alabama 1975.
Keep records on file:	6 Years.

ALASKA

Alaska Fuel Tax Refund Claim Instructions: Fuel tax refund for fuel purchased for charity-owned vehicles, construction equipment, fabrication, farming equipment, fuel exports, fire trucks, golf course equipment, government-owned vehicles, heating, logging equipment, mining equipment, off-road use, oilfield equipment, planes and public utility-owned equipment.

INSTRUCTIONS	
State the fuel is purchased in:	AK
Fuel type:	Gasoline, gasohol, jet fuel and undyed diesel fuel.
Refund type:	Aviation (foreign flights), charitable institutions, construction (off-highway refund), exports, fabrication, farming (off-highway refund), Federal and state government agencies, fire trucks, golf course equipment (off-highway refund), heating, logging, mining, off-road use, oilfield equipment (off-highway refund), public utilities, schools, snowmobiles, stationary equipment and stationary power plants.
Form name:	Various, see below.
Form #:	Required form(s): **04-544**, *Claim for Refund Template.* Additional forms required based on refund type: **04-544.1**, *Schedule of invoices for purchases.* **04.544.2**, *For non-highway purchases.* **04-544.3**, *For purchases of jet fuel for foreign flights.* **04.544.4**, *For jet fuel sold to carriers of foreign flights.* **04.544.5**, *For exports.*
Obtain required forms from:	http://www.tax.alaska.gov//programs/programs/forms/index.aspx?60210
Tax deducted from refund:	No.
Tax paid on separate return:	No.
Difficulty:	Moderate.
File by:	1 year from the date the fuel was purchased.
Attach documents to claim:	Copies of motor fuel receipts or invoices. Additional information may be requested.
Send to address:	Alaska Department of Revenue Tax Division P.O. Box 110420 Juneau, AK 99811-0420
Don't file if:	N/A.
State statute(s) supporting refund:	§ 43-40-030.
Keep records on file:	Indefinitely.

ARIZONA

<u>Arizona Fuel Tax Refund Claim Instructions</u>: Fuel tax refund for undyed diesel purchased for construction equipment, farming equipment, government-owned vehicles, golf course equipment, idling time, off-road use, PTO vehicles and reefer trailers.

INSTRUCTIONS	
State the fuel is purchased in:	AZ
Fuel type:	Undyed diesel fuel.
Refund type:	Construction equipment, Federal and state government agencies, farming, golf course equipment, idling time, off-road use, PTO (power take-off) vehicles and refrigeration (reefer) trailers.
Form name:	Various, see below.
Form #:	Required form(s): **96-0168,** *Use Fuel Refund Application.* Additional forms required based on fuel usage: **96-0161,** *Fuel Refund Equipment List.* **96-0168A,** *Use Fuel 26 cent Log Summary Schedule.* **96-0168B,** *Use Fuel 18 cent Log Summary Schedule.* **96-0168C,** *Bulk Use Fuel Log Summary Schedule.*
Obtain required forms from:	http://www.azdot.gov/mvd/motorcarrier/FuelTaxRefunds.asp
Tax deducted from refund:	Yes.
Tax paid on separate return:	No.
Difficulty:	Difficult.
File by:	Licensed filer - 3 Years from the date was purchased. Unlicensed filer - 6 months from the date the fuel purchased.
Attach documents to claim:	Copies of motor fuel receipts or invoices.
Send to address:	Arizona Department of Transportation Fuel Tax Refund Compliance Unit Mail Drop 521M P.O. Box 2100 Phoenix AZ 85001
Don't file if:	Sales tax is greater than refund.
State statute(s) supporting refund:	§ 42-5159.
Keep records on file:	3 years.

Arizona Fuel Tax Refund Claim Instructions: Fuel tax refund for fuel purchased for qualified IFTA vehicles declared on a filed IFTA return.

INSTRUCTIONS	
State the fuel is purchased in:	AZ
Fuel type:	Gasoline, gasohol, jet fuel and undyed diesel fuel.
Refund type:	IFTA carriers based outside AZ.
Form name:	*Foreign - Based IFTA Carrier Tax Credit Refund Application.*
Form #:	**96-0158.**
Obtain required forms from:	http://www.azdot.gov/mvd/motorcarrier/FuelTaxRefunds.asp
Tax deducted from refund:	No.
Tax paid on separate return:	No.
Difficulty:	Easy.
File by:	3 years after the original base jurisdiction IFTA report was required to be filed.
Attach documents to claim:	Copies of filed IFTA returns and IFTA licenses for reported periods.
Send to address:	Mail Drop 521M Fuel Tax Refund Compliance Unit AZ Dept. of Transportation P.O. Box 2100 Phoenix, AZ 85001-2100
Don't file if:	Refund is less than $50, unless 3 year statute is expiring.
State statute(s) supporting refund:	N/A.
Keep records on file:	3 years.

<u>Arizona Fuel Tax Refund Claim Instructions</u>: Undyed diesel tax refund for overpayment of fuel purchased.

INSTRUCTIONS	
State the fuel is purchased in:	AZ
Fuel type:	Undyed diesel fuel.
Refund type:	Overpayment on use fuel sold to light class motor vehicles or exempt use class motor vehicles.
Form name:	Various, see below.
Form #:	Required form(s): **96-0152**, *Use Fuel Vendor Refund Application.* **96-0152A**, *Use Fuel Vendor Summary Detail.* **96-0152B**, *Use Fuel Vendor Branch Worksheet.* **96-0152C**, *Vendor Use Fuel Log for Light Class / Exempt Use Class.* If you do not have a use fuel vendor license: **96-0492**, *Motor Fuel License Application*
Obtain required forms from:	http://www.azdot.gov/mvd/motorcarrier/FuelTaxRefunds.asp
Tax deducted from refund:	No.
Tax paid on separate return:	No.
Difficulty:	Moderate.
File by:	Licensed filer - 3 Years from the date was purchased. Unlicensed filer - 6 months from the date the fuel purchased.
Attach documents to claim:	Copies of motor fuel receipts or invoices.
Send to address:	Mail Drop 521M Fuel Tax Refund Compliance Unit AZ Dept. of Transportation P.O. Box 2100 Phoenix, AZ 85001-2100
Don't file if:	Refund is less than $50.00 for a calendar quarter, except when it is at least $10.00 during a three year period.
State statute(s) supporting refund:	§ 28-5725.
Keep records on file:	3 years.

<u>Arizona Fuel Tax Refund Claim Instructions</u>: Fuel tax refund for fuel exports.

INSTRUCTIONS	
State the fuel is purchased in:	AZ
Fuel type:	Gasoline, jet fuel and undyed diesel fuel.
Refund type:	Exports.
Form name:	Various, see below.
Form #:	Required form(s): **96-0159**, *Exporter Refund Application.* Additional forms required: **96-0159A**, *Exporter Refund Summary Schedule.* **96-0159B**, *Exporter Refund Worksheet.*
Obtain required forms from:	http://www.azdot.gov/mvd/motorcarrier/FuelTaxRefunds.asp
Tax deducted from refund:	No.
Tax paid on separate return:	No.
Difficulty:	Moderate.
File by:	6 months from date of purchase.
Attach documents to claim:	Copies of motor fuel receipts or invoices. Also include: A.) Bills of lading. B.) Fuel tax report destination state.
Send to address:	Mail Drop 521M Fuel Tax Refund Compliance Unit AZ Dept. of Transportation P.O. Box 2100 Phoenix, AZ 85001-2100
Don't file if:	N/A.
State statute(s) supporting refund:	§ 28-5610.
Keep records on file:	3 years.

<u>Arizona Fuel Tax Refund Claim Instructions</u>: Fuel tax refund for fuel purchased and used by Native Americans.

INSTRUCTIONS	
State the fuel is purchased in:	AZ
Fuel type:	Gasoline and undyed diesel fuel.
Refund type:	Native American-owned vehicles. Note: Vehicles must be leased or owned and operated for the sole benefit of a tribal government.
Form name:	Various, see below.
Form #:	Required form(s): **96-0225**, *Tribal Vehicle Fuel Refund Application.* **96-0225A**, *Tribal Government Fuel Log Summary Schedule.*
Obtain required forms from:	http://www.azdot.gov/mvd/motorcarrier/FuelTaxRefunds.asp
Tax deducted from refund:	No.
Tax paid on separate return:	No.
Difficulty:	Moderate.
File by:	6 months from date of purchase.
Attach documents to claim:	Copies of motor fuel receipts or invoices.
Send to address:	Mail Drop 521M Fuel Tax Refund Compliance Unit AZ Dept. of Transportation P.O. Box 2100 Phoenix, AZ 85001-2100
Don't file if:	Refund is less than $10.00 and a prior claim for less than $10.00 was filed in a 6 month period of time.
State statute(s) supporting refund:	§ 28-5610.
Keep records on file:	3 years.

Arizona Fuel Tax Refund Claim Instructions: Fuel tax refund for fuel purchased for planes.

INSTRUCTIONS	
State the fuel is purchased in:	AZ
Fuel type:	Jet fuel.
Refund type:	Aviation.
Form name:	Various, see below.
Form #:	Required form(s): **96-0466**, *Motor Vehicle / Aviation Fuel Refund Application.* **96-0466A**, *Motor Vehicle Fuel Log Summary Schedule.* **96-0466B**, *Aviation Fuel Log Summary Schedule.* **96-0161**, *Fuel Refund Equipment List.*
Obtain required forms from:	http://www.azdot.gov/mvd/motorcarrier/FuelTaxRefunds.asp
Tax deducted from refund:	No.
Tax paid on separate return:	No.
Difficulty:	Moderate.
File by:	Licensed filer - 3 Years from the date was purchased. Unlicensed filer - 6 months from the date the fuel purchased.
Attach documents to claim:	Copies of fuel receipts or invoices. Also include copies of flight logs.
Send to address:	Mail Drop 521M Fuel Tax Refund Compliance Unit AZ Dept. of Transportation P.O. Box 2100 Phoenix, AZ 85001-2100
Don't file if:	Refund is less than $10.00 and a prior claim for less than $10.00 was filed in a 6 month period of time.
State statute(s) supporting refund:	§ 28-5610.
Keep records on file:	3 years.

Arizona Fuel Tax Refund Claim Instructions: Fuel tax refund for fuel purchased and used by an enrolled member of a Native American tribe.

INSTRUCTIONS	
State the fuel is purchased in:	AZ
Fuel type:	Gasoline and undyed diesel fuel.
Refund type:	Native American-owned vehicle (Enrolled member of tribe). Note: Only for fuel purchased and used on the Indian Reservation.
Form name:	*Tribal Member Refund Application.*
Form #:	**96-0490.**
Obtain required forms from:	http://www.azdot.gov/mvd/motorcarrier/FuelTaxRefunds.asp
Tax deducted from refund:	No.
Tax paid on separate return:	No.
Difficulty:	Moderate.
File by:	6 months from the date of purchase.
Attach documents to claim:	Copies of motor fuel receipts or invoices.
Send to address:	Mail Drop 521M Fuel Tax Refund Compliance Unit AZ Dept. of Transportation P.O. Box 2100 Phoenix, AZ 85001-2100
Don't file if:	Refund is less than $10.00 and a prior claim for less than $10.00 was filed in a 6 month period of time.
State statute(s) supporting refund:	§ 28-5610.
Keep records on file:	3 years.

ARKANSAS

Arkansas Fuel Tax Refund Claim Instructions: Fuel tax refund for fuel purchased for volunteer fire department-owned vehicles.

INSTRUCTIONS	
State the fuel is purchased in:	AR
Fuel type:	Gasoline and undyed diesel fuel.
Refund type:	Volunteer fire department vehicles. Note: Qualified vehicles include pumper trucks, tanker trucks and equipment trucks.
Form name:	None.
Form #:	No form number. Requires filing a *Fire Department Refund Permit Application* on an initial claim.
Obtain required forms from:	Call Arkansas Motor Fuel Tax Section at (501) 682-4800.
Tax deducted from refund:	No.
Tax paid on separate return:	No.
Difficulty:	Easy.
File by:	The annual date for claiming a refund will be July 1st of each year. Refunds will be processed for purchases of fuel made 1 year prior to this refund date or date the license was issued.
Attach documents to claim:	Copies of motor fuel receipts or invoices. The filer will also need to provide the following: A.) The quantity of motor fuel and distillate special fuel purchased for use in its fire trucks. B.) A statement that the motor fuel and distillate special fuel have been used exclusively in its fire trucks. C.) The amount of the tax claimed to be refunded. D.) If the department has bulk storage capability, then a bulk invoice from the wholesale oil company must be obtained.
Send to address:	Arkansas Department of Revenue Motor Fuel Tax Section P.O. Box 1752 Little Rock, AR 72203
Don't file if:	N/A.
State statute(s) supporting refund:	§ 26-55-1303.
Keep records on file:	3 years.

CALIFORNIA

California Fuel Tax Refund Claim Instructions: Fuel tax refund for undyed diesel purchased for boats, farming equipment, off-road use, PTO vehicles and reefer trailers.

INSTRUCTIONS	
State the fuel is purchased in:	CA
Fuel type:	Undyed diesel fuel.
Refund type:	Boats, farming, Federal and state government agencies, off-road use, PTO (power take-off) vehicles and refrigeration (reefer) trailers.
Form name:	Various, see below.
Form #:	Required form(s): **BOE-770-DU**, *Diesel Fuel Claim for Refund on Nontaxable Uses.* **BOE 810-FTG**, *Receipt Schedule.* **BOE-810-FTF,** *Disbursement Schedule.* Additional forms required based on refund type: **13J**, *Tax-Paid Fuel Used in an Exempt Manner Not Reportable on Another Credit Schedule.* **13J5,** *Tax-Paid Fuel Used in Vessel.* **13J6**, *Tax-Paid Fuel Used in Construction Equipment Exempt from Registration Operated Off-Highway.* **13J7,** *Tax-Paid Fuel Used Off-Highway.* **13J8**, *Tax-Paid Fuel Used in The Operation of Power Take-Off Equipment.* **13J9,** *Tax-Paid Fuel Used in Vehicles Operated on Highways Under The Jurisdiction of the U.S. Department of Agriculture.*
Obtain required forms from:	http://www.boe.ca.gov/sptaxprog/sptaxforms.htm
Tax deducted from refund:	No.
Tax paid on separate return:	No.
Difficulty:	Difficult.
File by:	3 years from the date the fuel was purchased.
Attach documents to claim:	Copies of motor fuel receipts or invoices on your first claim only along with fuel tax refund calculation. On all other claims, submit copies upon request from California Board of Equalization. Additional documentation may be requested to support the claim.
Send to address:	California State Board of Equalization Motor Carrier Section 450 N. St. MIC 65 P.O. Box 942879 Sacramento, CA 94279
Don't file if:	Quarterly claim is less than $750.00.
State statute(s) supporting refund:	§ 8-1-60501.
Keep records on file:	4 years.

California Fuel Tax Refund Claim Instructions: Fuel tax refund for overpayment of fuel purchased.

INSTRUCTIONS	
State the fuel is purchased in:	CA
Fuel type:	Gasoline, gasohol, jet fuel and undyed diesel fuel.
Refund type:	Overpayment of excise tax by licensed suppliers and jet fuel dealers.
Form name:	*Claim for Refund or Credit.*
Form #:	**BOE-101.**
Obtain required forms from:	http://www.boe.ca.gov/sptaxprog/sptaxforms.htm
Tax deducted from refund:	No.
Tax paid on separate return:	No.
Difficulty:	Easy.
File by:	3 years from the date the fuel was purchased.
Attach documents to claim:	Copies of motor fuel receipts or invoices. Additional information may be required.
Send to address:	California State Board of Equalization Motor Carrier Section 450 N. St. MIC 65 P.O. Box 942879 Sacramento, CA 94279
Don't file if:	N/A.
State statute(s) supporting refund:	§ 8-2-60522.2.
Keep records on file:	4 years.

<u>California Fuel Tax Refund Claim Instructions</u>: Fuel tax refund for fuel purchased and used in farming, fuel exports and mass transit buses.

INSTRUCTIONS	
State the fuel is purchased in:	CA
Fuel type:	Gasoline.
Refund type:	Exports, farming and mass transit buses.
Form name:	*Gasoline Tax Refund Claim*.
Form #:	**SCGR-1.**
Obtain required forms from:	http://www.sco.ca.gov/Files-ARD-Tax-Info/gtr_forms_scgr-1.pdf
Tax deducted from refund:	No.
Tax paid on separate return:	No.
Difficulty:	Moderate.
File by:	3 years from the date the fuel was purchased. Can be filed annually or quarterly.
Attach documents to claim:	Copies of motor fuel receipts or invoices. Additional information such as fuel logs may be required.
Send to address:	California State Board of Equalization Motor Carrier Section 450 N. St. MIC 65 P.O. Box 942879 Sacramento, CA 94279
Don't file if:	Quarterly claim is less than $750.00.
State statute(s) supporting refund:	§ 7-1-8101.
Keep records on file:	4 years.

California Fuel Tax Refund Claim Instructions: Fuel tax refund for undyed diesel vendors for fuel used in farming, government-owned vehicles, fuel exports, mass transit buses and trains.

INSTRUCTIONS	
State the fuel is purchased in:	CA
Fuel type:	Undyed diesel fuel sold by vendors.
Refund type:	Exports, farming, state and Federal government agencies, mass transit buses and trains.
Form name:	Various, see below.
Form #:	Required form(s): **BOE-770-DV**, *Diesel Fuel Ultimate Vendor Report/Claim for Refund.* Use the following for calculations but do not include with your return: **13A**, *Tax-Paid Fuel Exported.* **13C**, *Tax-Paid Fuel Sold to the United States Government.* **13D**, *Tax-Paid Fuel Sold for Use on Farms.* **13E**, *Tax-Paid Fuel Sold to Exempt Bus Operators.* **13G**, *Tax-Paid Fuel Sold to Train Operators.*
Obtain required forms from:	http://www.boe.ca.gov/sptaxprog/sptaxforms.htm
Tax deducted from refund:	No.
Tax paid on separate return:	No.
Difficulty:	Difficult.
File by:	3 years from the date the fuel was purchased. Can be filed annually or quarterly.
Attach documents to claim:	N/A.
Send to address:	California State Board of Equalization Motor Carrier Section 450 N. St. MIC 65 P.O. Box 942879 Sacramento, CA 94279
Don't file if:	N/A.
State statute(s) supporting refund:	§ 8-1-60507.
Keep records on file:	4 years.

California Fuel Tax Refund Claim Instructions: Fuel tax credit for suppliers of undyed diesel fuel used in farming, mass transit, fuel exports, government-owned vehicles and trains.

INSTRUCTIONS	
State the fuel is purchased in:	CA
Fuel type:	Undyed diesel fuel sold by suppliers.
Refund type:	Exports, farming equipment, Federal and state government, bus operations and trains.
Form name:	Various, see below.
Form #:	Required form(s): **BOE-501-DD**, *Supplier of Diesel Fuel Tax Return.* Various schedules required. Please refer to refund claim form.
Obtain required forms from:	http://www.boe.ca.gov/sptaxprog/sptaxforms.htm
Tax deducted from refund:	No.
Tax paid on separate return:	No.
Difficulty:	Difficult.
File by:	3 years from the date the fuel was purchased.
Attach documents to claim:	All applicable schedules and the *Tax Computation Worksheet.*
Send to address:	California State Board of Equalization Motor Carrier Section 450 N. St. MIC 65 P.O. Box 942879 Sacramento, CA 94279
Don't file if:	N/A.
State statute(s) supporting refund:	§ 8-2-60522.
Keep records on file:	4 years.

California Fuel Tax Refund Claim Instructions: Fuel tax credit for undyed diesel fuel purchased for school buses and government-owned vehicles.

INSTRUCTIONS	
State the fuel is purchased in:	CA
Fuel type:	Undyed diesel fuel.
Refund type:	School buses, state and Federal government agencies.
Form name:	*Government Entity Diesel Fuel Tax Return.*
Form #:	**BOE-501-DG.**
Obtain required forms from:	http://www.boe.ca.gov/sptaxprog/sptaxforms.htm
Tax deducted from refund:	No.
Tax paid on separate return:	No.
Difficulty:	Moderate.
File by:	3 years from the date the fuel was purchased.
Attach documents to claim:	None.
Send to address:	California State Board of Equalization Motor Carrier Section 450 N. St. MIC 65 P.O. Box 942879 Sacramento, CA 94279
Don't file if:	N/A.
State statute(s) supporting refund:	§ 8-2-60522.
Keep records on file:	4 years.

California Fuel Tax Refund Claim Instructions: Fuel tax refund for fuel vendors for undyed diesel fuel sold for government-owned vehicles, off-road use and trains. Additional refund applicability includes fuel sold to be exported.

INSTRUCTIONS	
State the fuel is purchased in:	CA
Fuel type:	Undyed diesel fuel sold by vendor.
Refund type:	Exports, off- highway use, state and Federal government agencies and trains.
Form name:	Various, see below.
Form #:	Required form(s): **BOE-770-DZ**, Claim for Refund on Nontaxable Sales and Exports of Diesel Fuel Additional forms required based on refund type: **13A**, *Tax-Paid Fuel Exported* **13C**, *Tax-Paid Fuel Sold to the United States Government* **13G**, *Tax-Paid Fuel Sold to Train Operators*
Obtain required forms from:	http://www.boe.ca.gov/sptaxprog/sptaxforms.htm
Tax deducted from refund:	No.
Tax paid on separate return:	No.
Difficulty:	Moderate.
File by:	3 years from the date the fuel was purchased.
Attach documents to claim:	None.
Send to address:	California State Board of Equalization Motor Carrier Section 450 N. St. MIC 65 P.O. Box 942879 Sacramento, CA 94279
Don't file if:	Quarterly claim is less than $750.00.
State statute(s) supporting refund:	§ 8-1-60507.
Keep records on file:	4 years.

California Fuel Tax Refund Claim Instructions: Fuel tax credit for fuel purchased for various off-road and out-of-state purposes.

INSTRUCTIONS	
State the fuel is purchased in:	CA
Fuel type:	State alcohol fuels containing not more than 15 percent gasoline, CNG (compressed natural gas), distillate , ethanol, kerosene, LNG (liquefied natural gas), LPG (liquefied petroleum gas), methanol and stove oil.
Refund type:	Credit for farming equipment and off-road use. Other: Credit for fuel used in the tanks of motor vehicles operated outside of CA. Other: Credit for LPG, LNG, CNG in vehicles for which annual flat tax rate has been paid.
Form name:	*User Use Fuel Tax Return.*
Form #:	**BOE-501-AU.**
Obtain required forms from:	http://www.boe.ca.gov/sptaxprog/sptaxforms.htm
Tax deducted from refund:	No.
Tax paid on separate return:	No.
Difficulty:	Difficult.
File by:	3 years from the date the fuel was purchased.
Attach documents to claim:	N/A.
Send to address:	California State Board of Equalization Motor Carrier Section 450 N. St. MIC 65 P.O. Box 942879 Sacramento, CA 94279
Don't file if:	N/A.
State statute(s) supporting refund:	§ 6-1-9151.
Keep records on file:	4 years.

California Fuel Tax Refund Claim Instructions: Fuel tax credit for fuel purchased and used for school and local transit purposes.

INSTRUCTIONS	
State the fuel is purchased in:	CA
Fuel type:	State alcohol fuels containing not more than 15 percent gasoline, CNG (compressed natural gas), distillate , ethanol, kerosene, LNG (liquefied natural gas), LPG (liquefied petroleum gas), methanol and stove oil.
Refund type:	Bus operators and common carriers (operating exclusively within the limits of a single city between fixed terminals or over a regular route, 98 percent of whose operations are within the limits of a single city).
Form name:	*Exempt Bus Operator Use Fuel Tax Return.*
Form #:	**BOE-501-AB.**
Obtain required forms from:	http://www.boe.ca.gov/sptaxprog/sptaxforms.htm
Tax deducted from refund:	Yes.
Tax paid on separate return:	No.
Difficulty:	Difficult.
File by:	3 years from the date the fuel was purchased.
Attach documents to claim:	Schedules for auditing purposes.
Send to address:	California State Board of Equalization Motor Carrier Section 450 N. St. MIC 65 P.O. Box 942879 Sacramento, CA 94279
Don't file if:	Do not include fuel used on any route which exceeds 50 miles one-way.
State statute(s) supporting refund:	§ 6-1-9151.
Keep records on file:	4 years unless BOE states otherwise.

COLORADO

Colorado Fuel Tax Refund Claim Instructions: Fuel tax refund for fuel purchased for boats, farming equipment, cleaning, dyeing, government-owned vehicles, off-road use, planes, PTO vehicles, school-owned vehicles, reefer trailers and trains.

INSTRUCTIONS	
State the fuel is purchased in:	CO
Fuel type:	Gasoline, gasohol, jet fuel and undyed diesel fuel.
Refund type:	Aviation, cleaning, commercial boat use, dyeing, farming, off-road use, refrigeration (reefer) trailers, schools, state and Federal government agencies, stationary engines and trains
Form name:	*Fuel Tax Refund Claim.*
Form #:	**DR 7118.**
Obtain required forms from:	http://www.colorado.gov/cs/Satellite/Revenue/REVX/1176829278920
Tax deducted from refund:	No.
Tax paid on separate return:	No.
Difficulty:	Easy.
File by:	1 year from the date the fuel was purchased.
Attach documents to claim:	The claim may be submitted without fuel purchase invoices.
Send to address:	Colorado Department of Revenue Taxpayer Service Division Special Tax Section 1375 Sherman St., Rm. 200 Denver, CO 80261
Don't file if:	Claim is for less than 20 gallons. This limitation does not apply to governmental agencies or political subdivisions.
State statute(s) supporting refund:	§39-27-103(3)(a), C.R.S.
Keep records on file:	3 years.

<u>Colorado Fuel Tax Return Credit Instructions</u>: Fuel tax return credit for fuel exports.

INSTRUCTIONS	
State the fuel is purchased in:	CO
Fuel type:	Blend components, gasoline, gasohol, jet fuel and undyed diesel fuel.
Refund type:	Exports.
Form name:	Various, see below.
Form #:	Required form(s): **DR 7055**, *Distributor Schedule of Receipts Worksheet.* **DR 7056**, *Distributor Schedule of Disbursements Worksheet.* **DR 7056**, *Distributor Schedule of Disbursements Worksheet.*
Obtain required forms from:	The filer must have a signed *COFTS Electronic Trading Partner Agreement* on file. Additional information concerning the electronic filing using COFTS is available at www.cofts.com. Additional help may be received by calling (720) 962-4569 or (877) 352-2586.
Tax deducted from refund:	No.
Tax paid on separate return:	No.
Difficulty:	Easy.
File by:	Monthly.
Attach documents to claim:	The claim may be submitted without fuel purchase invoices.
Send to address:	Colorado Department of Revenue Taxpayer Service Division Special Tax Section 1375 Sherman St., Rm. 200 Denver, CO 80261
Don't file if:	N/A.
State statute(s) supporting refund:	N/A.
Keep records on file:	3 years.

CONNECTICUT

Connecticut Fuel Tax Refund Claim Instructions: Fuel tax refund for fuel purchased for boats, government-owned vehicles, off-road vehicles, PTO vehicles and school-owned vehicles.

INSTRUCTIONS	
State the fuel is purchased in:	CT
Fuel type:	Gasoline, gasohol and undyed diesel fuel.
Refund type:	Commercial boating, off-road use, state and Federal government agencies and school buses. Other: Waste Hauling only for CRRA Mid-Connecticut Project.
Form name:	*Special Fuel Tax Return.*
Form #:	**AU-724.**
Obtain required forms from:	http://www.ct.gov/drs/cwp/view.asp?a=1509&q=449724#mvftr
Tax deducted from refund:	Yes.
Tax paid on separate return:	No.
Difficulty:	Moderate.
File by:	On or before May 31th, for fuel used during the preceding calendar year.
Attach documents to claim:	Copies of motor fuel receipts or invoices.
Send to address:	Connecticut Department of Revenue Services State of Connecticut Excise Taxes Unit 25 Sigourney St., Ste. 2 Hartford CT 06106
Don't file if:	Sales tax is greater than refund, or if the claim is for less than 200 gallons.
State statute(s) supporting refund:	§ 12-459.
Keep records on file:	3 years.

Connecticut Fuel Tax Refund Claim Instructions: Fuel tax refund for fuel purchased for farming equipment.

INSTRUCTIONS	
State the fuel is purchased in:	CT
Fuel type:	Gasoline, gasohol and undyed diesel fuel.
Refund type:	Farming equipment.
Form name:	*Motor Vehicle Fuels Tax Refund Claim.*
Form #:	**AU-725.**
Obtain required forms from:	http://www.ct.gov/drs/cwp/view.asp?a=1509&q=449724#mvftr
Tax deducted from refund:	Yes.
Tax paid on separate return:	No.
Difficulty:	Moderate.
File by:	On or before May 31th, for fuel used during the preceding calendar year.
Attach documents to claim:	Copies of motor fuel receipts or invoices and a copy of the current *Farmer Tax Exemption Permit.*
Send to address:	Connecticut Department of Revenue Services State of Connecticut Excise Taxes Unit 25 Sigourney St., Ste. 2 Hartford CT 06106
Don't file if:	Sales tax is greater than refund, or if the claim is for less than 200 gallons.
State statute(s) supporting refund:	§ 12-459.
Keep records on file:	3 years.

Connecticut Fuel Tax Refund Claim Instructions: Fuel tax refund for fuel purchased for mass transit buses, taxis and livery vehicles.

INSTRUCTIONS	
State the fuel is purchased in:	CT
Fuel type:	Gasoline, gasohol and undyed diesel fuel.
Refund type:	Mass transit buses, livery vehicles and taxis.
Form name:	*Motor Vehicle Fuels Tax Refund Claim.*
Form #:	**AU-736.**
Obtain required forms from:	http://www.ct.gov/drs/cwp/view.asp?a=1509&q=449724#mvftr
Tax deducted from refund:	No.
Tax paid on separate return:	No.
Difficulty:	Moderate.
File by:	On or before May 31th, for fuel used during the preceding calendar year.
Attach documents to claim:	Copies of motor fuel receipts or invoices.
Send to address:	Connecticut Department of Revenue Services State of Connecticut Excise Taxes Unit 25 Sigourney St., Ste. 2 Hartford CT 06106
Don't file if:	Claim is for less than 200 gallons.
State statute(s) supporting refund:	§ 12-459.
Keep records on file:	3 years.

<u>Connecticut Fuel Tax Refund Claim Instructions</u>: Fuel tax refund for fuel purchased for airport service motor buses.

INSTRUCTIONS	
State the fuel is purchased in:	CT
Fuel type:	Gasoline, gasohol and undyed diesel fuel.
Refund type:	Airport service motor buses.
Form name:	*Motor Vehicle Fuels Tax Refund Claim.*
Form #:	**AU-737.**
Obtain required forms from:	http://www.ct.gov/drs/cwp/view.asp?a=1509&q=449724#mvftr
Tax deducted from refund:	No.
Tax paid on separate return:	No.
Difficulty:	Moderate.
File by:	On or before May 31th, for fuel used during the preceding calendar year.
Attach documents to claim:	Copies of motor fuel receipts or invoices. Motor bus companies must attach a copy of their *Certificate of Public Convenience and Necessity.*
Send to address:	Connecticut Department of Revenue Services State of Connecticut Excise Taxes Unit 25 Sigourney St., Ste. 2 Hartford CT 06106
Don't file if:	Claim is for less than 200 gallons.
State statute(s) supporting refund:	§ 12-459.
Keep records on file:	3 years.

Connecticut Fuel Tax Refund Claim Instructions: Fuel tax refund for fuel purchased for Meals on Wheels use.

INSTRUCTIONS	
State the fuel is purchased in:	CT
Fuel type:	Gasoline, gasohol and undyed diesel fuel.
Refund type:	Meals on Wheels.
Form name:	*Motor Vehicle Fuels Tax Refund Claim.*
Form #:	**AU-738.**
Obtain required forms from:	http://www.ct.gov/drs/cwp/view.asp?a=1509&q=449724#mvftr
Tax deducted from refund:	No.
Tax paid on separate return:	No.
Difficulty:	Moderate.
File by:	On or before May 31th, for fuel used during the preceding calendar year.
Attach documents to claim:	Copies of motor fuel receipts or invoices.
Send to address:	Connecticut Department of Revenue Services State of Connecticut Excise Taxes Unit 25 Sigourney St., Ste. 2 Hartford CT 06106
Don't file if:	Claim is for less than 200 gallons.
State statute(s) supporting refund:	§ 12-459.
Keep records on file:	3 years.

<u>Connecticut Fuel Tax Refund Claim Instructions</u>: Fuel tax refund for fuel purchased for commuter van usage.

INSTRUCTIONS	
State the fuel is purchased in:	CT
Fuel type:	Gasoline, gasohol and undyed diesel fuel.
Refund type:	Commuter vans.
Form name:	*Motor Vehicle Fuels Tax Refund Claim.*
Form #:	**AU-741.**
Obtain required forms from:	http://www.ct.gov/drs/cwp/view.asp?a=1509&q=449724#mvftr
Tax deducted from refund:	No.
Tax paid on separate return:	No.
Difficulty:	Moderate.
File by:	On or before May 31th, for fuel used during the preceding calendar year.
Attach documents to claim:	Copies of motor fuel receipts or invoices.
Send to address:	Connecticut Department of Revenue Services State of Connecticut Excise Taxes Unit 25 Sigourney St., Ste. 2 Hartford CT 06106
Don't file if:	Claim is for less than 200 gallons.
State statute(s) supporting refund:	§ 12-459.
Keep records on file:	3 years.

Connecticut Fuel Tax Refund Claim Instructions: Fuel tax credit for fuel purchased for export usage.

INSTRUCTIONS	
State the fuel is purchased in:	CT
Fuel type:	Undyed diesel fuel.
Refund type:	Exports.
Form name:	Various, see below.
Form #:	Required form(s): **OP-216**, *Special Fuel Tax Return.* **O-MF**, *Motor Vehicle Fuels Tax Return.*
Obtain required forms from:	http://www.ct.gov/drs/cwp/view.asp?a=1509&q=449724#mvftr
Tax deducted from refund:	No.
Tax paid on separate return:	No.
Difficulty:	Moderate.
File by:	Monthly.
Attach documents to claim:	The fuel tax return may be submitted without fuel purchase invoices.
Send to address:	Connecticut Department of Revenue Services State of Connecticut Excise Taxes Unit 25 Sigourney St., Ste. 2 Hartford CT 06106
Don't file if:	N/A.
State statute(s) supporting refund:	§ 12-455A (C) AND 12-458.
Keep records on file:	3 years.

D.C., WASHINGTON

Washington D.C. Fuel Tax Return Claim Instructions: Fuel tax return credit for fuel exports.

INSTRUCTIONS	
State the fuel is purchased in:	DC
Fuel type:	Undyed diesel fuel.
Refund type:	Exports.
Form name:	*Motor Fuel Tax Return.*
Form #:	**FR-400M**.
Obtain required forms from:	http://otr.cfo.dc.gov/otr/cwp/view,a,1330,q,647286.asp#tax12
Tax deducted from refund:	No.
Tax paid on separate return:	No.
Difficulty:	Moderate.
File by:	Monthly. File your return by and pay any tax due by the 25th of the month following the month being reported.
Attach documents to claim:	The fuel tax return may be submitted without fuel purchase invoices.
Send to address:	Office of Tax and Revenue Audit Division P.O. Box 556 Washington, DC 20044-0556
Don't file if:	N/A.
State statute(s) supporting refund:	DC ST § 47-2309.
Keep records on file:	3 years.

DELAWARE

<u>Delaware Fuel Tax Refund Claim Instructions</u>: Fuel tax refund for gasoline purchased for construction equipment, farming equipment, planes, stationary equipment and taxis.

INSTRUCTIONS	
State the fuel is purchased in:	DE
Fuel type:	Gasoline.
Refund type:	Commercial boating, construction equipment, farming, planes, stationary equipment and taxis.
Form name:	*Application for Motor Fuel (Gasoline) Tax Refund.*
Form #:	**MFT-4.**
Obtain required forms from:	http://www.deldot.gov/mfta/gasoline_refund_program.shtml
Tax deducted from refund:	No.
Tax paid on separate return:	No.
Difficulty:	Difficult.
File by:	1 year from the date the fuel was purchased.
Attach documents to claim:	Original motor fuel receipts or invoices marked "paid" and initialed by the seller, or proof of payment must be attached.
Send to address:	State of Delaware Motor Fuel Tax Administration P.O. Drawer E. Dover, DE 19903
Don't file if:	N/A.
State statute(s) supporting refund:	30 Del C c. 51 §5120, and Section G of the Promulgated Regulation.
Keep records on file:	4 years.

Delaware Fuel Tax Refund Claim Instructions: Fuel tax credit for fuel purchased for exports.

INSTRUCTIONS	
State the fuel is purchased in:	DE
Fuel type:	Various.
Refund type:	Exports.
Form name:	*State of Delaware Motor Fuel Tax Administration Licensed Motor Fuel Distributor Tax Return.*
Form #:	**MFT-1.**
Obtain required forms from:	http://deldot.gov/mfta/pdf/distributor_return_cover_sheet_062107.pdf
Tax deducted from refund:	No.
Tax paid on separate return:	No.
Difficulty:	Difficult.
File by:	Monthly.
Attach documents to claim:	No documentation required.
Send to address:	State of Delaware Motor Fuel Tax Administration P.O. Drawer E. Dover, DE 19903
Don't file if:	N/A.
State statute(s) supporting refund:	30 Del C c. 51 §5120, and Section G of the Promulgated Regulation.
Keep records on file:	4 years.

FLORIDA

Florida Fuel Tax Refund Claim Instructions: Fuel tax refund for gasoline purchased for commercial boat use, farming and planes.

INSTRUCTIONS	
State the fuel is purchased in:	FL
Fuel type:	Gasoline.
Refund type:	Commercial boating, farming equipment and planes.
Form name:	Various, see below.
Form #:	Required form(s): **DR-138**, *Application for Fuel Tax Refund.* **DR-185,** *Application for Fuel Tax Refund Permit.* This application must be filed to be eligible for the refund. The Florida Department of Revenue may require a corporate surety bond of $1,000 with the application for any person who violated an applicable provision of § 206-41, or was convicted of bribery, theft, or false swearing within the preceding five years, or if the Department has evidence of the applicant's financial irresponsibility.
Obtain required forms from:	Call Florida Department of Revenue at (850) 617-8585.
Tax deducted from refund:	No.
Tax paid on separate return:	No.
Difficulty:	Difficult.
File by:	The last day of the first month following the quarter for which the refund is claimed.
Attach documents to claim:	Motor fuel receipts or invoices.
Send to address:	Florida Department of Revenue Refunds Subprocess P.O. Box 6490 Tallahassee FL 32314
Don't file if:	Claim is less than $5.00 for any given period.
State statute(s) supporting refund:	§ 14-206-64, 14-206-42.
Keep records on file:	3 years.

Florida Fuel Tax Refund Claim Instructions: Fuel tax refund for fuel purchased for fixed-route mass transit buses.

INSTRUCTIONS	
State the fuel is purchased in:	FL
Fuel type:	Biodiesel, gasoline and undyed diesel fuel.
Refund type:	Licensed mass transit operators who offer fixed routes to the public.
Form name:	Various, see below.
Form #:	Monthly: **DR-309633**, *Monthly Mass Transit System Provider Fuel Tax Return.* Quarterly: **DR-160**, *Quarterly Application for Fuel Tax Refund–Mass Transit System Users.*
Obtain required forms from:	Call Florida Department of Revenue at (850) 617-8585.
Tax deducted from refund:	Yes, but not on state and Federal government agencies.
Tax paid on separate return:	No.
Difficulty:	Moderate.
File by:	The 20th day of the month following the collection period. If the 20th is a Saturday, Sunday, state holiday, or Federal holiday, your return and payment must be received or postmarked on the next business day, even if no tax is due.
Attach documents to claim:	Keep original invoices, fuel logs, and equipment lists on file in the event of an audit.
Send to address:	Florida Department of Revenue 5050 W Tennessee Street Tallahassee, FL 32399-0100
Don't file if:	N/A.
State statute(s) supporting refund:	§ 14-206-874.
Keep records on file:	3 years.

<u>Florida Fuel Tax Refund Claim Instructions</u>: Fuel tax refund for fuel purchased for government-owned vehicles and school-owned equipment.

INSTRUCTIONS	
State the fuel is purchased in:	FL
Fuel type:	Gasoline and undyed diesel fuel.
Refund type:	Local government (municipality, county and school district) agencies.
Form name:	Various, see below.
Form #:	**DR-309634**, *Local Government User of Diesel Fuel Tax Return.* **DR-189,** *Quarterly Application for Fuel Tax Refund – Municipalities, Counties and School Districts.*
Obtain required forms from:	Call Florida Department of Revenue at (850) 617-8585.
Tax deducted from refund:	Yes.
Tax paid on separate return:	No.
Difficulty:	Moderate.
File by:	A return indicating an overpayment of tax must be filed within 3 years from the date tax was originally paid.
Attach documents to claim:	Original invoices or certified copies of invoices must be retained and made available upon request. Schedules are reviewed for out of date purchases and duplicate transactions. Taxpayers are required to submit exemption certificates if applicable.
Send to address:	Florida Department of Revenue 5050 W Tennessee Street Tallahassee, FL 32399-0100
Don't file if:	N/A.
State statute(s) supporting refund:	§ 14-206-874.
Keep records on file:	3 years.

<u>Florida Fuel Tax Refund Claim Instructions</u>: Fuel tax refund for fuel purchased for non-public schools.

INSTRUCTIONS	
State the fuel is purchased in:	FL
Fuel type:	Gasoline and undyed diesel fuel.
Refund type:	Non-public schools.
Form name:	*Application for Fuel Tax Refund (Non-public schools).*
Form #:	**DR-190.**
Obtain required forms from:	Call Florida Department of Revenue at (850) 617-8585.
Tax deducted from refund:	No.
Tax paid on separate return:	No.
Difficulty:	Moderate.
File by:	3 years from the date the fuel was purchased.
Attach documents to claim:	Copies of motor fuel receipts or invoices.
Send to address:	Florida Department of Revenue Refunds Subprocess P.O. Box 6490 Tallahassee FL 32314
Don't file if:	N/A.
State statute(s) supporting refund:	§ 14-206-874.
Keep records on file:	3 years.

Florida Fuel Tax Refund Claim Instructions: Fuel tax refund for fuel purchased for cooking, heating, construction equipment, off-road use, PTO vehicles, reefer trailers and stationary equipment.

INSTRUCTIONS	
State the fuel is purchased in:	FL
Fuel type:	Undyed diesel fuel.
Refund type:	Commercial cooking, heating, construction equipment, off-road use, PTO (power take-off) equipment, refrigeration (reefer) trailers and stationary equipment.
Form name:	*Application for Refund of Tax Paid on Undyed Diesel Used for Off-road or Other Exempt Purposes.*
Form #:	**DR-309639.**
Obtain required forms from:	http://dor.myflorida.com/dor/forms/
Tax deducted from refund:	Yes.
Tax paid on separate return:	No.
Difficulty:	Difficult.
File by:	3 years from the date the fuel was purchased.
Attach documents to claim:	Copies of motor fuel receipts or invoices.
Send to address:	Refund Subprocess Florida Department of Revenue P.O. Box 6490 Tallahassee FL 32314-6490
Don't file if:	Sales tax is greater than refund.
State statute(s) supporting refund:	§ 14-206-8745.
Keep records on file:	3 years.

Florida Fuel Tax Refund Claim Instructions: Fuel tax refund for fuel purchased for specific mass transit purposes.

INSTRUCTIONS	
State the fuel is purchased in:	FL
Fuel type:	Undyed diesel fuel.
Refund type:	Mass transit vehicles and buses. Note: Equipment muse be privately owned, designed to carry nine or more passengers, has a gross vehicle weight of at least 33,000 pounds, used exclusively in the commercial application of transporting passengers for compensation and has the capacity to measure diesel fuel consumed in Florida during idling separate from diesel fuel consumed to propel the vehicle, by way of an on-board computer.
Form name:	*Application for Refund of Tax Paid on Undyed Diesel Consumed by Motor Coaches During Idle Time in Florida.*
Form #:	**DR-309640.**
Obtain required forms from:	http://dor.myflorida.com/dor/forms/
Tax deducted from refund:	Yes.
Tax paid on separate return:	No.
Difficulty:	Moderate.
File by:	The annual refund claim must be submitted before April 1 of the year following the year in which the tax was paid.
Attach documents to claim:	Copies of motor fuel receipts or invoices.
Send to address:	Florida Department of Revenue Refunds Subprocess P.O. Box 6490 Tallahassee FL 32314
Don't file if:	Sales tax is greater than refund.
State statute(s) supporting refund:	§ 14-206-8745.
Keep records on file:	3 years.

Florida Fuel Tax Refund Claim Instructions: Fuel pollutants tax refund for fuel purchased and used for coastal protection.

INSTRUCTIONS	
State the fuel is purchased in:	FL
Fuel type:	Any fuel purchased for coastal protection, water quality, and inland protection purposes.
Refund type:	Tax-paid petroleum products exported from the state or bunkered into a marine vessel engaged in interstate or foreign commerce by a licensed terminal supplier, importer, exporter, producer, wholesaler or dealer.
Form name:	*Application for Pollutants Tax Refund.*
Form #:	**DR-309660.**
Obtain required forms from:	http://dor.myflorida.com/dor/forms/
Tax deducted from refund:	No.
Tax paid on separate return:	No.
Difficulty:	Moderate.
File by:	Claim must be filed quarterly, no later than the last day of the month immediately following the end of the quarter. The filing date may be extended 1 additional month only if a justified excuse is submitted in writing and the prior quarter's application was filed timely.
Attach documents to claim:	Copies of fuel receipts or invoices.
Send to address:	Florida Department of Revenue Refunds Subprocess P.O. Box 6490 Tallahassee FL 32314
Don't file if:	Claim is less than $5.00 for any given period.
State statute(s) supporting refund:	§ 14-206-9942.
Keep records on file:	3 years.

Florida Fuel Tax Refund Claim Instructions: Fuel tax refund for fuel purchased for planes.

INSTRUCTIONS	
State the fuel is purchased in:	FL
Fuel type:	Jet fuel.
Refund type:	Planes.
Form name:	Various, see below.
Form #:	Required form(s): **DR-191**, *Application for Aviation Fuel Refund - Air Carrier.* **UCT-6**, *Employer's Quarterly Tax Report - Florida Department of Revenue.* **Schedule 1A**, *Schedule of Purchases of Tax-Paid Aviation Fuel.*
Obtain required forms from:	http://dor.myflorida.com/dor/forms/
Tax deducted from refund:	No.
Tax paid on separate return:	No.
Difficulty:	Easy.
File by:	Claim must be filed quarterly, no later than the last day of the month immediately following the end of the quarter. The filing date may be extended 1 additional month only if a justified excuse is submitted in writing and the prior quarter's application was filed timely.
Attach documents to claim:	Copies of fuel receipts or invoices.
Send to address:	Distribution Center Florida Department of Revenue 5050 W Tennessee St Tallahassee FL 32399-0100
Don't file if:	N/A.
State statute(s) supporting refund:	§ 14-206-9855.
Keep records on file:	3 years.

GEORGIA

Georgia Fuel Tax Refund Claim Instructions: Fuel tax refund for fuel purchased for government-owned vehicles, off-road use and racing vehicles.

INSTRUCTIONS	
State the fuel is purchased in:	GA
Fuel type:	Undyed diesel fuel.
Refund type:	Off-road use, racing vehicles, state and Federal government agencies.
Form name:	*Application for Motor Fuel Tax Refund, Non-Highway Use of Taxable Clear Diesel Fuel.*
Form #:	**MFR-43**.
Obtain required forms from:	https://etax.dor.ga.gov/motorfuel/motor_fuel_tax_unit_forms.aspx
Tax deducted from refund:	No.
Tax paid on separate return:	No.
Difficulty:	Easy.
File by:	18 months from the date the fuel was purchased.
Attach documents to claim:	Copies of motor fuel receipts or invoices. In order for any person to be eligible for the refund provided by this Code section, the person must obtain a refund permit issued by the commissioner.
Send to address:	Georgia Department of Revenue Motor Fuel Tax Unit Refund Section 1800 Century Center Blvd. NE.,Ste. 8223 Atlanta, GA 30345
Don't file if:	N/A.
State statute(s) supporting refund:	O.C.G.A. § 48-9-10.
Keep records on file:	3 years.

<u>Georgia Fuel Tax Refund Claim Instructions</u>: Fuel tax refund for overpayment of tax by distributor.

INSTRUCTIONS	
State the fuel is purchased in:	GA
Fuel type:	Gasoline and undyed diesel fuel.
Refund type:	Overpayment by distributor.
Form name:	Various, see below.
Form #:	Required form(s): **MFD-33** , *Licensed Distributor application for Refund.* **ST-12A**, *Waiver of Vendors Rights.*
Obtain required forms from:	https://etax.dor.ga.gov/motorfuel/ motor_fuel_tax_unit_forms.aspx
Tax deducted from refund:	No.
Tax paid on separate return:	No.
Difficulty:	Easy.
File by:	6 months from the date the fuel was purchased.
Attach documents to claim:	Copies of motor fuel receipts or invoices.
Send to address:	Georgia Department of Revenue Motor Fuel Tax Unit Refund Section 1800 Century Center Blvd NE Suite 8223 Atlanta, GA 30345-3205
Don't file if:	N/A.
State statute(s) supporting refund:	O.C.G.A. § 48-9-10.
Keep records on file:	3 years.

<u>Georgia Fuel Tax Refund Claim Instructions</u>: Fuel tax credit for distributors of fuel for exports, government-owned vehicles and planes.

INSTRUCTIONS	
State the fuel is purchased in:	GA
Fuel type:	Alcohol, biodiesel, CNG (compressed natural gas), gasoline, gasohol, jet fuel, kerosene, LNG (liquid natural gas), petroleum and undyed diesel fuel.
Refund type:	Exports, planes, state and Federal government agencies.
Form name:	*Motor Fuel Tax Report.*
Form #:	**MFD-04.**
Obtain required forms from:	https://etax.dor.ga.gov/motorfuel/motor_fuel_tax_unit_forms.aspx
Tax deducted from refund:	No.
Tax paid on separate return:	No.
Difficulty:	Difficult.
File by:	20th day of the month following month of purchase.
Attach documents to claim:	Copies of motor fuel receipts or invoices.
Send to address:	Georgia Department of Revenue Motor Fuel Tax Unit Refund Section 1800 Century Center Blvd NE Suite 8223 Atlanta, GA 30345-3205
Don't file if:	N/A.
State statute(s) supporting refund:	O.C.G.A. § 48-9-10.
Keep records on file:	3 years.

HAWAII

<u>Hawaii Fuel Tax Refund Claim Instructions</u>: Fuel tax refund for fuel purchased for boats, construction equipment, farming equipment, heating, off-road use and stationary equipment.

INSTRUCTIONS	
State the fuel is purchased in:	HI
Fuel type:	Biodiesel, CNG (compressed natural gas), gasoline, ethanol, LNG (liquefied natural gas), LPG (liquefied petroleum gas), methanol and undyed diesel fuel.
Refund type:	Construction equipment, commercial boat use, farming, heating, off-road use, stationary equipment, state and Federal government agencies.
Form name:	*Combined Claim for Refund of Fuel Taxes*.
Form #:	**M-36.**
Obtain required forms from:	http://www.state.hi.us/tax/a1_b3_5fuel.htm
Tax deducted from refund:	No.
Tax paid on separate return:	No.
Difficulty:	Moderate.
File by:	On or before the 20th day of the month following the close of the filing period. If the due date falls on a Saturday, Sunday, or legal holiday, file by the next regular workday. All claims are to be filed on a calendar year basis. However, claims exceeding $1,000 within any calendar quarter or claims exceeding $1,000 within two or more calendar quarters may be filed quarterly.
Attach documents to claim:	Copies of motor fuel receipts or invoices.
Send to address:	State of Hawaii Department of Taxation P.O. Box 259 Honolulu, Hawaii 96809
Don't file if:	N/A.
State statute(s) supporting refund:	§ 243-4(a), 243-4(b), 243-4(c), 243-7(a), Hawaii Revised Statutes (HRS). § 18-243-4-01 and 18-243-4-02, Hawaii Administrative Rules (HAR). Tax Facts 99-1.
Keep records on file:	5 years.

<u>Hawaii Fuel Tax Return Claim Instructions</u>: Income tax credit for fuel purchased for commercial fishing.

INSTRUCTIONS	
State the fuel is purchased in:	HI
Fuel type:	Ethanol and undyed diesel fuel.
Refund type:	Commercial fishing.
Form name:	*Fuel Tax Credit For Commercial Fishers.*
Form #:	**N-163.** Attach this schedule to form N-11, N-15, N-20, N-30, N-35, N-40, or N-70NP.
Obtain required forms from:	No.
Tax deducted from refund:	No.
Tax paid on separate return:	http://www.state.hi.us/tax/a1_b3_5fuel.htm
Difficulty:	Moderate.
File by:	Claims for the credit, including any amended claims thereof, must be filed on or before the end of the 12th month following the close of the indicated taxable year.
Attach documents to claim:	N/A.
Send to address:	State of Hawaii Department of Taxation P.O. Box 259 Honolulu, Hawaii 96809
Don't file if:	N/A.
State statute(s) supporting refund:	§ 243-4(a), 243-4(b), 243-4(c), 243-7(a), Hawaii Revised Statutes (HRS). § 18-243-4-01 and 18-243-4-02, Hawaii Administrative Rules (HAR). Tax Facts 99-1.
Keep records on file:	5 years.

IDAHO

Idaho Fuel Tax Refund Claim Instructions: Fuel tax refund for fuel purchased for ATVs, boats, government-owned vehicles, heating, off-road use, planes, PTO vehicles, reefer trailers, stationary equipment and trains.

INSTRUCTIONS	
State the fuel is purchased in:	ID
Fuel type:	Aviation gas, CNG (compressed natural gas), gasoline, jet fuel, propane, LNG (liquid natural gas) and undyed diesel fuel.
Refund type:	For CNG, LNG, propane and undyed diesel: Commercial boating, heating, off-road use, planes, refrigeration (reefer) trailers, PTO (power take-off) equipment, state and Federal government agencies and stationary equipment. For gasoline: Commercial boating, off-road use, planes, refrigeration (reefer) trailers, stationary equipment and unregistered ATVs (all-terrain vehicles).
Form name:	Various, see below.
Form #:	Required Forms(s): **Form 75**, *Idaho Fuels Use Report.* **Form 75-BST**, *Idaho Fuels Tax Refund Worksheet.* If you use a bulk-storage tank for non-taxable purposes. **Form 75-IMV**, *Idaho Fuels Tax Refund Worksheet - Intrastate Motor Vehicles.* If you are claiming a refund on in-state vehicles that utilize special fuels. **Form 75-IC**, *Idaho Fuels Tax Refund Worksheet-IFTA Licensees.* If you are claiming a refund on PTO equipment. **Form 75-LFA**, *Idaho Fuels Tax Refund Worksheet - Line Flush Allowance.* If you are a distributor claiming a refund on contaminated fuel.
Obtain required forms from:	http://tax.idaho.gov/s-results-form.cfm
Tax deducted from refund:	Yes, if no exemption from the Idaho sales and use tax.
Tax paid on separate return:	No.
Difficulty:	Difficult.
File by:	3 years from the date the fuel was purchased.
Attach documents to claim:	Copies of motor fuel receipts or invoices.
Send to address:	Idaho State Tax Commission P.O. Box 76 Boise, ID 83707
Don't file if:	Claim is for less than 50 gallons of gasoline or undyed diesel.
State statute(s) supporting refund:	§ 63-2410, 63-2423.
Keep records on file:	3 years.

ILLINOIS

<u>Illinois Fuel Tax Refund Claim Instructions</u>: Fuel tax refund for fuel purchased and used in boats, construction equipment, accidental fuel contamination, farming equipment, industrial use, lawn equipment, manufacturing, off-road vehicles, planes, PTO vehicles, R&D, reefer trailers, government-owned vehicles, testing and trains.

INSTRUCTIONS	
State the fuel is purchased in:	IL
Fuel type:	Gasoline, LPG (liquid petroleum gas) and undyed diesel fuel.
Refund type:	Construction equipment, farming equipment, fuel unintentionally mixed with dyed diesel, industrial equipment, lawn equipment, loss, manufacturing equipment, marine, off-road, planes, PTO (power take-off equipment), R&D (research and development), refrigeration (reefer) trailers, state and Federal government agencies, testing and trains.
Form name:	*Illinois Motor Fuel Tax Refund Claim.*
Form #:	**RMFT-11-A.**
Obtain required forms from:	http://tax.illinois.gov/TaxForms/Misc/Mft/index.htm
Tax deducted from refund:	No.
Tax paid on separate return:	No.
Difficulty:	Difficult.
File by:	Unlicensed distributor or supplier: 2 years ago or less. Licensed distributors and suppliers: 1 year ago or less.
Attach documents to claim:	Please send original refund claim, plus one copy along with copies of motor fuel receipts or invoices. Additional information may be required.
Send to address:	Motor Fuel Tax Refund Illinois Department of Revenue P.O. Box 19019 Springfield, IL 62794
Don't file if:	N/A.
State statute(s) supporting refund:	35 ILCS 505/13 (from Ch. 120, par. 429, Sec. 13).
Keep records on file:	3 years.

INDIANA

<u>Indiana Fuel Tax Return Credit Instructions</u>: Biodiesel fuel tax credit for biodiesel fuel purchased.

INSTRUCTIONS	
State the fuel is purchased in:	IN
Fuel type:	Biodiesel fuel.
Refund type:	Producers, blenders, retailers of biodiesel fuel.
Form name:	*Biodiesel Tax Credits Application.*
Form #:	**BD-100.**
Obtain required forms from:	http://www.in.gov/dor/3512.htm
Tax deducted from refund:	No.
Tax paid on separate return:	No.
Difficulty:	Easy.
File by:	Any unused credit can be carried forward for up to 6 years on at least one return or until all credits have been used.
Attach documents to claim:	The Biodiesel Credits can be applied as a credit against the following tax returns. A copy of the approved **BD-100** must be attached to the return. The credit can be entered on the following tax returns: A.) Sales and Use Tax Return (§ 6-2.5). B.) Adjusted Gross Income Tax Return (§ 6-3-1, 6-3-7). C.) Financial Institution Tax Return (§ 6-5.5). D.) Insurance Premium Tax Return (§ 27-1-18-2).
Send to address:	Indiana Department of Revenue Tax Administration P.O. Box 6197 Indianapolis, IN 46204
Don't file if:	N/A.
State statute(s) supporting refund:	§ 6-3.1-27.
Keep records on file:	4 years.

<u>Indiana Fuel Tax Refund Claim Instructions</u>: Sales tax credit for fuel used in specialty metered pumps in Indiana for a tax-exempt purpose.

INSTRUCTIONS	
State the fuel is purchased in:	IN
Fuel type:	Gasoline, gasohol, LPG (liquefied petroleum gas), CNG (compressed natural gas) compressed methane, propane and undyed diesel fuel.
Refund type:	Any equipment fueled from stationary metered pumps in Indiana for a tax exempt purpose.
Form name:	*Claim for Refund - Sales Tax on Gasoline, Gasohol, & Special Fuel Dispensed through Stationary Metered Pumps in Indiana.*
Form #:	http://www.in.gov/dor/3512.htm
Obtain required forms from:	**GA-110LMP**.
Tax deducted from refund:	No.
Tax paid on separate return:	No.
Difficulty:	Moderate.
File by:	No statute specified.
Attach documents to claim:	Attach original Form **STR-100**, *Certification of Exempt Purchases of Gasoline & Special Fuel* or copies of each receipt.
Send to address:	Indiana Department of Revenue 100 N. Senate Avenue, Room N203 Indianapolis, IN 46204
Don't file if:	N/A.
State statute(s) supporting refund:	§ 6-2.5-7-2.
Keep records on file:	4 years.

<u>Indiana Fuel Tax Refund Claim Instructions</u>: Fuel tax refund for fuel purchased for common carrier vehicles, commercial boating, construction equipment, exports, farming equipment, heating, industrial equipment, manufacturing, mass transit, mining, planes, taxis, off-road use, PTO vehicles, reefer trailers and trains.

INSTRUCTIONS	
State the fuel is purchased in:	IN
Fuel type:	Gasoline, gasohol and undyed diesel fuel.
Refund type:	Agricultural equipment, common carrier, commercial boating, construction equipment, exports, heating, industrial equipment, off-road equipment, mass transit, planes, taxis, maintenance equipment, mining, manufacturing, PTO (power take-off) equipment, refrigeration (reefer) trailers and trains.
Form name:	Various, see below.
Form #:	**REF-1000,** *Consolidated Application for Fuel Tax Refund.* **REF-1000A,** *Affidavit of Certification of Tax Paid Invoices.*
Obtain required forms from:	http://www.in.gov/dor/3512.htm
Tax deducted from refund:	Yes.
Tax paid on separate return:	No.
Difficulty:	Moderate.
File by:	Undyed Fuel (3 years after fuel was purchased). Gasoline (Must be filed by April 15th of the year succeeding 3 years after the date the gasoline was purchased).
Attach documents to claim:	Original Invoices or copies of invoices.
Send to address:	Indiana Department of Revenue Special Tax Section P. O. Box 1971 Indianapolis, IN 46206-1971
Don't file if:	Sales tax is greater than refund.
State statute(s) supporting refund:	§ 6-6-2.5-30.
Keep records on file:	4 years.

IOWA

Iowa Fuel Tax Refund Claim Instructions: Fuel tax refund for fuel purchased for commercial boating, contract carrier usage, denaturing alcohol, extraction, exports, farming, government-owned vehicles, heating, idling, manufacturing, mass transit buses, Native American-owned equipment, off-road use, PTO vehicles, pumping dry and wet product, ready mix usage, reefer trailers, processing solid waste and school buses.

INSTRUCTIONS	
State the fuel is purchased in:	IA
Fuel type:	Alcohol, aviation gas, E85, gasoline, gasohol, LPG (liquid petroleum gas) and undyed diesel fuel.
Refund type:	Commercial boating, commercial fishing, contract carrier, denaturing alcohol, extract/process natural deposits, exports, farming equipment, heating, idling, state and Federal government agencies, mass transit buses, Native American-owned equipment, refrigeration (reefer) trailer, pumping dry product, pumping wet product, PTO (power take-off equipment), off-road use, public school buses, ready mix use and solid waste use. Note: **Contract Carrier** is a carrier who has a contract with a public school under Iowa Code section 285.5 for transporting students.
Form name:	*Iowa Motor Fuel / Special Fuel Tax Refund Worksheet.*
Form #:	**82-052a.** Note: The form should contain a series of prompts that allow the filer to file the claim via telephone.
Obtain required forms from:	Call (515) 242-6033 or (515) 281-6447 to obtain this refund form.
Tax deducted from refund:	Yes.
Tax paid on separate return:	No.
Difficulty:	Moderate.
File by:	3 years from the date the fuel was purchased.
Attach documents to claim:	The claim may be submitted without fuel purchase invoices.
Send to address:	Iowa Dept. of Revenue Motor Fuel Unit Examination Section P.O. Box 10456 Des Moines, IA 50306
Don't file if:	Sales tax is greater than refund.
State statute(s) supporting refund:	§ 155-24-452A.17, Code 1995.
Keep records on file:	3 years.

<u>Iowa Fuel Tax Return Credit Instructions</u>: Sales tax credit for biodiesel fuel producers.

<table>
<tr><th colspan="2">INSTRUCTIONS</th></tr>
<tr><td>State the fuel is purchased in:</td><td>IA</td></tr>
<tr><td>Fuel type:</td><td>Biodiesel fuel.</td></tr>
<tr><td>Refund type:</td><td>Biodiesel producers may apply for a refund of the amount of sales or use tax imposed and paid upon purchases made by the person.
• The person must be engaged in the manufacturing of biodiesel and must have registered with the U.S. environmental protection agency as a manufacturer of biodiesel.
• The biodiesel manufactured must be used in biodiesel blended fuel.
• The Department will refund the amount claimed after subtracting any amount of Iowa sales or use tax imposed and paid upon purchases by the biodiesel producer.</td></tr>
<tr><td>Form name:</td><td>Claim for Refund Sales, Use, Excise, and Local Option Tax.</td></tr>
<tr><td>Form #:</td><td>IA 843.</td></tr>
<tr><td>Obtain required forms from:</td><td>Call (515) 242-6033 or (515) 281-6447 to obtain this refund form.</td></tr>
<tr><td>Tax deducted from refund:</td><td>Yes.</td></tr>
<tr><td>Tax paid on separate return:</td><td>No.</td></tr>
<tr><td>Difficulty:</td><td>Moderate.</td></tr>
<tr><td>File by:</td><td>3 years from the date the fuel was purchased.</td></tr>
<tr><td>Attach documents to claim:</td><td>Motor fuel receipts or invoices.</td></tr>
<tr><td>Send to address:</td><td>Iowa Dept. of Revenue
Motor Fuel Unit
Examination Section
P.O. Box 10456
Des Moines, IA 50306</td></tr>
<tr><td>Don't file if:</td><td>No refund will be allowed on gallons produced in excess of 25 million at a facility during each of the calendar years 2012 to 2014. No refund will be allowed for gallons produced at a facility on or after January 1, 2015.</td></tr>
<tr><td>State statute(s) supporting refund:</td><td>§ 12-701-12.18 (423).</td></tr>
<tr><td>Keep records on file:</td><td>3 years.</td></tr>
</table>

<u>Iowa Fuel Tax Return Credit Instructions</u>: Ethanol income tax credit for ethanol fuel sold.

INSTRUCTIONS	
State the fuel is purchased in:	IA
Fuel type:	E15 plus gasoline (Gasoline with an ethanol content of at least 15%, but less than 70%).
Refund type:	Income tax credit on E15 plus gasoline available to retailers who sell fuel through motor fuel pumps in Iowa. • The tax credit rate is three cents per gallon for calendar years 2012-2014, and two cents per gallon for calendar years 2015-2017. • Any tax credit in excess of the tax liability is refundable.
Form name:	*E15 Plus Gasoline Promotion Tax Credit.*
Form #:	**IA 138** (Attach a copy to Iowa individual or corporate income tax return).
Obtain required forms from:	http://iowa.gov/tax/forms/corpinc.html
Tax deducted from refund:	No.
Tax paid on separate return:	No.
Difficulty:	Moderate.
File by:	3 years from the date the fuel was purchased.
Attach documents to claim:	The **IA 148**, *Tax Credits Schedule* must be completed.
Send to address:	Iowa Dept. of Revenue Motor Fuel Unit Examination Section P.O. Box 10456 Des Moines, IA 50306
Don't file if:	Tax credit is repealed after January 1, 2018.
State statute(s) supporting refund:	§ 422.11Y and 422.33(11D).
Keep records on file:	3 years.

<u>Iowa Fuel Tax Return Credit Instructions</u>: Ethanol income tax credit for retailers of ethanol-blended gasoline.

INSTRUCTIONS	
State the fuel is purchased in:	IA
Fuel type:	Ethanol-blended gasoline (such as E10, E85) sold by dealers.
Refund type:	Ethanol promotion tax credit is available to taxpayers who are: • Retail dealers of ethanol blended gasoline. • Operate motor fuel pumps at an Iowa retail motor fuel site. Tank wagons are considered retail motor fuel sites.
Form name:	*Ethanol Promotion Tax Credit.*
Form #:	**IA 137**. Note: Attach a copy to Iowa individual or corporate income tax return.
Obtain required forms from:	http://iowa.gov/tax/forms/corpinc.html
Tax deducted from refund:	No.
Tax paid on separate return:	No.
Difficulty:	Moderate.
File by:	3 years from the date the fuel was purchased.
Attach documents to claim:	None.
Send to address:	Iowa Dept. of Revenue Motor Fuel Unit Examination Section P.O. Box 10456 Des Moines, IA 50306
Don't file if:	N/A.
State statute(s) supporting refund:	§ 422.11N and 422.33(11A).
Keep records on file:	3 years.

Iowa Fuel Tax Return Credit Instructions: Biodiesel income tax credit for biodiesel-blended fuel sold.

INSTRUCTIONS	
State the fuel is purchased in:	IA
Fuel type:	Biodiesel-blended fuel sold by dealers.
Refund type:	Biodiesel blended tax credit is available to taxpayers who are: • Retail dealers of ethanol blended biodiesel. • Operate motor fuel pumps at an Iowa retail motor fuel site. Tank wagons are considered retail motor fuel sites.
Form name:	*Biodiesel Blended Fuel Tax Credit.*
Form #:	**IA 8864**. Note: Attach a copy to Iowa individual or corporate income tax.
Obtain required forms from:	http://iowa.gov/tax/forms/corpinc.html
Tax deducted from refund:	No.
Tax paid on separate return:	No.
Difficulty:	Moderate.
File by:	3 years from the date the fuel was purchased.
Attach documents to claim:	None.
Send to address:	Iowa Dept. of Revenue Motor Fuel Unit Examination Section P.O. Box 10456 Des Moines, IA 50306
Don't file if:	Less than 50 percent of the total gallons of diesel fuel sold by the dealer through motor fuel pumps in Iowa is biodiesel fuel containing a minimum percentage of two percent by volume of biodiesel.
State statute(s) supporting refund:	§ 422.11P and 422.33(11C)
Keep records on file:	3 years.

<u>Iowa Fuel Tax Return Credit Instructions</u>: E85 income tax credit for retailers of E85 gasoline.

INSTRUCTIONS	
State the fuel is purchased in:	IA
Fuel type:	E85 gasoline fuel sold by dealers.
Refund type:	E85 gasoline tax credit is available to taxpayers who are: • Retail dealers of E85 gasoline. • Operate motor fuel pumps at an Iowa retail motor fuel site. Tank wagons are considered retail motor fuel sites.
Form name:	Various, see below.
Form #:	**IA 135,** *E85 gasoline sold on or after January 1, 2006* (Attach a copy to Iowa individual or corporate income tax). **IA 148,** *Tax Credits Schedule.*
Obtain required forms from:	http://iowa.gov/tax/forms/corpinc.html
Tax deducted from refund:	No.
Tax paid on separate return:	No.
Difficulty:	Moderate.
File by:	3 years from the date the fuel was purchased.
Attach documents to claim:	N/A.
Send to address:	Iowa Dept. of Revenue Motor Fuel Unit Examination Section P.O. Box 10456 Des Moines, IA 50306
Don't file if:	The E85 gasoline has less than 70 percent volume of ethanol.
State statute(s) supporting refund:	§ 422.11O and 422.33(11B).
Keep records on file:	3 years.

KANSAS

Kansas Fuel Tax Refund Claim Instructions: Fuel tax refund for fuel purchased for biodiesel usage, boats, charity-owned vehicles, construction equipment, fabrication, farming equipment, fire trucks, golf course equipment, logging, mining, oilfield equipment, off-road use, PTO vehicles, public utility equipment, racing vehicles, school buses, stationary equipment, snowmobiles, trains and waste hauling equipment.

INSTRUCTIONS	
State the fuel is purchased in:	KS
Fuel type:	Gasoline, gasohol, E85, undyed diesel and biodiesel fuel.
Refund type:	Biodiesel use, charitable organization, commercial boating, construction equipment, fabrication, farming equipment, fire department, golf course equipment, logging, mining, off-road use, oilfield equipment, PTO (power take-off) equipment, public utility equipment, racing equipment, schools, stationary equipment, snowmobiles, trains and waste hauling.
Form name:	N/A.
Form #:	N/A.
Obtain required forms from:	Request proper form from Kansas DOR.
Tax deducted from refund:	Yes.
Tax paid on separate return:	No.
Difficulty:	Easy.
File by:	1 year from purchase.
Attach documents to claim:	Application required if a first-time filer: MF-51 (Application For Motor Fuel/Special Fuel Tax Refund Permit) for $6.00.
Send to address:	Kansas Department of Revenue Docking State Office Bldg., Motor Fuel 915 SW. Harrison St. Topeka, KS 66625
Don't file if:	N/A.
State statute(s) supporting refund:	K.S.A. § 79-3401, 8-128, 79-3453, 79-3454. Revenue Ruling 19-2004-02.
Keep records on file:	3 years.

KENTUCKY

Kentucky Fuel Tax Refund Claim Instructions: Fuel tax and environmental assurance fee refund for fuel purchased and used in farming equipment and off-road usage.

INSTRUCTIONS	
State the fuel is purchased in:	KY
Fuel type:	Gasoline and undyed diesel.
Refund type:	Farming equipment and off-road use.
Form name:	Various, see below.
Form #:	Required form(s): **72A053-A**, *Application For Refund of Kentucky Motor Fuel Tax Paid on Non-Highway Motor Fuels.* Note: The filer will have to file a bond with the Kentucky Department of Revenue. Please call for directions.
Obtain required forms from:	http://revenue.ky.gov/forms/curmftfrms.htm
Tax deducted from refund:	Yes, unless filer holds an *Energy Direct Pay Authorization* form, or uses fuel for agricultural purposes.
Tax paid on separate return:	No.
Difficulty:	Moderate.
File by:	4 years from the date the fuel was purchased.
Attach documents to claim:	Original motor fuel receipts or invoices.
Send to address:	Kentucky Department of Revenue Motor Fuels Tax Compliance Section P.O. Box 1303 Station 63 Frankfort, KY 40602
Don't file if:	Sales tax is greater than refund or fuel was purchased from retail filling station.
State statute(s) supporting refund:	KRS § 138.344 through 138.355.
Keep records on file:	4 years.

Kentucky Fuel Tax Refund Claim Instructions: Fuel tax refund for fuel purchased for commercial boating.

INSTRUCTIONS	
State the fuel is purchased in:	KY
Fuel type:	Gasoline and undyed diesel.
Refund type:	Commercial boating.
Form name:	Various, see below.
Form #:	**72A006**, *Motor Fuel Tax Refund Application*. Note: the filer will have to file a bond with the Kentucky Department of Revenue.
Obtain required forms from:	http://revenue.ky.gov/forms/curmftfrms.htm
Tax deducted from refund:	No.
Tax paid on separate return:	No.
Difficulty:	Difficult.
File by:	4 years from the date the fuel was purchased.
Attach documents to claim:	Original motor fuel receipts or invoices.
Send to address:	Kentucky Department of Revenue Motor Fuels Tax Compliance Section P.O. Box 1303 Station 63 Frankfort, KY 40602
Don't file if:	N/A.
State statute(s) supporting refund:	KRS § 138.445.
Keep records on file:	4 years.

<u>Kentucky Fuel Tax Refund Claim Instructions</u>: Fuel tax refund for fuel purchased and used in planes.

INSTRUCTIONS	
State the fuel is purchased in:	KY
Fuel type:	Gasoline.
Refund type:	Aviation.
Form name:	Various, see below.
Form #:	**72A066**, *Application For Refund of Kentucky Tax Paid on Gasoline Use in Operation of Aircraft.* Note: the filer will have to file a bond with the Kentucky Department of Revenue.
Obtain required forms from:	http://revenue.ky.gov/forms/curmftfrms.htm
Tax deducted from refund:	No.
Tax paid on separate return:	No.
Difficulty:	Difficult.
File by:	4 years from the date the fuel was purchased.
Attach documents to claim:	Original motor fuel receipts or invoices.
Send to address:	Kentucky Department of Revenue Motor Fuels Tax Compliance Section P.O. Box 1303 Station 63 Frankfort, KY 40602
Don't file if:	N/A.
State statute(s) supporting refund:	KRS § 138.341 to 138.342.
Keep records on file:	4 years.

Kentucky Fuel Tax Refund Claim Instructions: Fuel tax refund for fuel purchased for mass transit buses and taxis.

INSTRUCTIONS	
State the fuel is purchased in:	KY
Fuel type:	Gasoline and undyed diesel.
Refund type:	Mass transit buses and taxis.
Form name:	Various, see below.
Form #:	**72A072**, *Application For Motor Fuel Refund.* Note: the filer will have to file a bond with the Kentucky Department of Revenue.
Obtain required forms from:	http://revenue.ky.gov/forms/curmftfrms.htm
Tax deducted from refund:	No.
Tax paid on separate return:	No.
Difficulty:	Difficult.
File by:	4 years from the date the fuel was purchased.
Attach documents to claim:	Original motor fuel receipts or invoices.
Send to address:	Kentucky Department of Revenue Motor Fuels Tax Compliance Section P.O. Box 1303 Station 63 Frankfort, KY 40602
Don't file if:	N/A.
State statute(s) supporting refund:	KRS § 138.446.
Keep records on file:	4 years.

LOUISIANA

Louisiana Fuel Tax Refund Claim Instructions: Fuel tax refund for fuel purchased for off-road use.

INSTRUCTIONS	
State the fuel is purchased in:	LA
Fuel type:	Undyed diesel or undyed kerosene.
Refund type:	Off-road use.
Form name:	Various, see below.
Form #:	Required form(s): **R-5015**, *Claim for Refund of Tax on Undyed Diesel.* **R-5377**, *Registration Application for Diesel Fuels Refund–Users* (Must be completed and a certificate issued from the Department before the clear kerosene or diesel fuel is purchased).
Obtain required forms from:	http://revenue.louisiana.gov/sections/taxforms/ default.aspx?code=EXC&year=2011
Tax deducted from refund:	No.
Tax paid on separate return:	No.
Difficulty:	Difficult.
File by:	Within 30 days following the end of the quarter when the fuel was purchased.
Attach documents to claim:	Copies of motor fuel receipts or invoices. Additional information may be required.
Send to address:	Louisiana Department of Revenue Taxpayer Services Division Excise Tax Section P.O. Box 66362 Baton Rouge, LA 70896
Don't file if:	N/A.
State statute(s) supporting refund:	RS § 47-802.1.
Keep records on file:	4 years.

<u>Louisiana Fuel Tax Refund Claim Instructions</u>: Fuel tax refund for fuel purchased for commercial boating.

INSTRUCTIONS	
State the fuel is purchased in:	LA
Fuel type:	Gasoline and undyed diesel fuel.
Refund type:	Commercial boating.
Form name:	Various, see below.
Form #:	Required form(s): Tax Refund Claim (call for claim). **R-5330**, *Registration for Fuel Tax Refund for Commercial Fishermen* (Must be completed and a certificate issued from the Department before the gasoline or diesel fuel is purchased).
Obtain required forms from:	http://revenue.louisiana.gov/sections/taxforms/default.aspx?code=EXC&year=2011
Tax deducted from refund:	No.
Tax paid on separate return:	No.
Difficulty:	Difficult.
File by:	Within 6 months after the date of purchase.
Attach documents to claim:	Copies of motor fuel receipts or invoices. Additional information may be required.
Send to address:	Louisiana Department of Revenue Taxpayer Services Division Excise Tax Section P.O. Box 66362 Baton Rouge, LA 70896
Don't file if:	N/A.
State statute(s) supporting refund:	RS § 47-681.
Keep records on file:	4 years.

Louisiana Fuel Tax Refund Claim Instructions: Fuel tax refund for fuel purchased for planes.

INSTRUCTIONS	
State the fuel is purchased in:	LA
Fuel type:	Gasoline.
Refund type:	Aviation.
Form name:	Various, see below.
Form #:	Required form(s): Tax Refund Claim (call for claim). **R-5329**, *Gasoline Tax Refund Registration for Operators of Aircraft*. Must be completed and a certificate issued from the Department before the gasoline or diesel fuel is purchased.
Obtain required forms from:	http://revenue.louisiana.gov/sections/taxforms/default.aspx?code=EXC&year=2011
Tax deducted from refund:	No.
Tax paid on separate return:	No.
Difficulty:	Difficult.
File by:	Within 6 months after the date of purchase.
Attach documents to claim:	Copies of motor fuel receipts or invoices. Additional information may be required.
Send to address:	Louisiana Department of Revenue Taxpayer Services Division Excise Tax Section P.O. Box 66362 Baton Rouge, LA 70896
Don't file if:	N/A.
State statute(s) supporting refund:	RS § 47-716.1.
Keep records on file:	4 years.

Louisiana Fuel Tax Refund Claim Instructions: Fuel tax refund for gasoline purchased for farming equipment.

INSTRUCTIONS	
State the fuel is purchased in:	LA
Fuel type:	Gasoline.
Refund type:	Farming equipment.
Form name:	Various, see below.
Form #:	Required form(s): Tax Refund Claim (call for claim). **R-5328**, *Registration for Gasoline Tax Refund for Farmers*. Must be completed and a certificate issued from the Department before the gasoline is purchased.
Obtain required forms from:	http://revenue.louisiana.gov/sections/taxforms/default.aspx?code=EXC&year=2011
Tax deducted from refund:	No.
Tax paid on separate return:	No.
Difficulty:	Difficult.
File by:	Within 6 months after the date of purchase.
Attach documents to claim:	Copies motor fuel receipts or invoices. Additional information may be required.
Send to address:	Louisiana Department of Revenue Taxpayer Services Division Excise Tax Section P.O. Box 66362 Baton Rouge, LA 70896
Don't file if:	N/A.
State statute(s) supporting refund:	RS § 47-1681.
Keep records on file:	4 years.

Louisiana Fuel Tax Refund Claim Instructions: Fuel tax refund for fuel purchased for fuel exports.

INSTRUCTIONS	
State the fuel is purchased in:	LA
Fuel type:	Gasoline, gasohol, jet fuel and undyed diesel fuel.
Refund type:	Exports.
Form name:	*Distributor/Exporter/Blender Monthly Return.*
Form #:	**R-5398.**
Obtain required forms from:	http://revenue.louisiana.gov/sections/taxforms/default.aspx?code=EXC&year=2011
Tax deducted from refund:	No.
Tax paid on separate return:	No.
Difficulty:	Difficult.
File by:	20th day of the month following the period covered.
Attach documents to claim:	In order to receive credit or refund of Louisiana fuel taxes/inspection fees paid, an official certification of taxes paid to the receiving state must accompany the return for the period in which the gallons are claimed. Complete and attach Schedule E (Form **R-5292**) listing the exportations and evidencing the payment to the receiving state of the tax on the gallons exported. The exporter must be licensed within Louisiana to apply for this refund.
Send to address:	Louisiana Department of Revenue Taxpayer Services Division Excise Tax Section P.O. Box 66362 Baton Rouge, LA 70896
Don't file if:	N/A.
State statute(s) supporting refund:	RS § 47-811.
Keep records on file:	4 years.

Louisiana Fuel Tax Refund Claim Instructions: Fuel tax refund for fuel purchased and contaminated (fuel loss).

INSTRUCTIONS	
State the fuel is purchased in:	LA
Fuel type:	Gasoline, gasohol, jet fuel and undyed diesel fuel.
Refund type:	Loss.
Form name:	*Claim for Refund of Taxes Paid.*
Form #:	**R-20127-L.**
Obtain required forms from:	http://revenue.louisiana.gov/sections/taxforms/ default.aspx?code=EXC&year=2011
Tax deducted from refund:	No.
Tax paid on separate return:	No.
Difficulty:	Difficult.
File by:	After 3 years from the 31st day of December of the year in which the tax became due or after one year from the date the tax was paid, whichever is later.
Attach documents to claim:	Copies of motor fuel receipts or invoices. The filer will also need to provide the following: A.) Notarized statement certifying that the tax was paid on the clear fuel at the time purchased.
Send to address:	Louisiana Department of Revenue Taxpayer Services Division Excise Tax Section P.O. Box 66362 Baton Rouge, LA 70896
Don't file if:	N/A.
State statute(s) supporting refund:	RS § 47-1621.
Keep records on file:	4 years.

MAINE

<u>Maine Fuel Tax Refund Claim Instructions</u>: Fuel tax refund for fuel purchased for commercial boating, farming equipment, golf course equipment, idling, industrial equipment, mechanical equipment, off-road use, PTO vehicles, snowmobiles, stationary equipment and trains.

INSTRUCTIONS	
State the fuel is purchased in:	ME
Fuel type:	Gasoline and undyed diesel fuel.
Refund type:	Commercial boating, farming equipment, golf equipment, idling, industrial equipment, mechanical equipment, off-road use, PTO (power take-off) equipment, snowmobiles, stationary equipment and trains.
Form name:	*Maine Revenue Services Special Fuel and Gasoline Tax Refund Application.*
Form #:	**OFF-1.**
Obtain required forms from:	http://www.maine.gov/revenue/forms/fuel/fueltaxforms.htm
Tax deducted from refund:	Yes.
Tax paid on separate return:	No.
Difficulty:	Moderate.
File by:	1 year from the date the fuel was purchased.
Attach documents to claim:	Copies of motor fuel receipts or invoices.
Send to address:	Maine Revenue Service P.O. Box 1065 Augusta, ME 04332-1064
Don't file if:	Sales tax is greater than refund.
State statute(s) supporting refund:	36 §2903.
Keep records on file:	6 years.

<u>Maine Fuel Tax Refund Claim Instructions</u>: Fuel tax refund for fuel purchased for planes.

INSTRUCTIONS	
State the fuel is purchased in:	ME
Fuel type:	Gasoline and aviation fuel.
Refund type:	Planes.
Form name:	*Aviation Gasoline Refund Application.*
Form #:	**AVG.**
Obtain required forms from:	http://www.maine.gov/revenue/forms/fuel/fueltaxforms.htm
Tax deducted from refund:	Yes.
Tax paid on separate return:	No.
Difficulty:	Moderate.
File by:	1 year from the date the fuel was purchased.
Attach documents to claim:	Copies of motor fuel receipts or invoices.
Send to address:	Maine Revenue Service P.O. Box 1064 Augusta, ME 04332-1064
Don't file if:	Sales tax is greater than refund.
State statute(s) supporting refund:	36 §2910.
Keep records on file:	6 years.

<u>Maine Fuel Tax Refund Claim Instructions</u>: Fuel tax refund for fuel purchased and used by the government.

INSTRUCTIONS	
State the fuel is purchased in:	ME
Fuel type:	Biodiesel, gasoline and undyed diesel fuel.
Refund type:	State and Federal government agencies.
Form name:	*Political Subdivision Fuel Tax Refund Application.*
Form #:	**Sub.**
Obtain required forms from:	http://www.maine.gov/revenue/forms/fuel/fueltaxforms.htm
Tax deducted from refund:	No.
Tax paid on separate return:	No.
Difficulty:	Moderate.
File by:	1 year from the date the fuel was purchased.
Attach documents to claim:	Include the following: • Copies of motor fuel receipts or invoices. • A copy of the *Political Subdivision Affidavit for Assignment of Refund.* • *A* copy of the contract between the Agency the Political Subdivision of the State and the third party must be filed with Maine Revenue Services. No refunds will be issued to third parties without the proper documentation on file.
Send to address:	Maine Revenue Service P.O. Box 1064 Augusta, ME 04332-1064
Don't file if:	N/A.
State statute(s) supporting refund:	36 §3208-A.
Keep records on file:	6 years.

<u>Maine Fuel Tax Refund Claim Instructions</u>: Fuel tax refund for fuel purchased for heating, cooking, exports, power generation, resale and government-owned vehicles.

INSTRUCTIONS	
State the fuel is purchased in:	ME
Fuel type:	Kerosene, propane, natural gas and undyed diesel.
Refund type:	Heating, cooking, state and Federal government agencies, resale, exports and power generation.
Form name:	*Maine Revenue Services Special Fuel Supplier/Retailer Tax Return.*
Form #:	**SFS.**
Obtain required forms from:	http://www.maine.gov/revenue/forms/fuel/fueltaxforms.htm
Tax deducted from refund:	No.
Tax paid on separate return:	No.
Difficulty:	Moderate.
File by:	1 year from the date the fuel was purchased.
Attach documents to claim:	None.
Send to address:	Maine Revenue Service P.O. Box 1064 Augusta, ME 04332-1064
Don't file if:	Copies of motor fuel receipts or invoices.
State statute(s) supporting refund:	36 §3204-A.
Keep records on file:	6 years.

<u>Maine Fuel Tax Refund Claim Instructions</u>: Fuel tax refund for gasoline purchased and used for government-owned vehicles and planes. Further refund application exists for fuel distribution and exports.

INSTRUCTIONS	
State the fuel is purchased in:	ME
Fuel type:	Gasoline.
Refund type:	Aviation (International Flights), sales to licensed distributors, state and Federal government agencies and exports.
Form name:	*Maine Revenue Services Special Fuel Supplier/Retailer Tax Return.*
Form #:	**GAS.**
Obtain required forms from:	http://www.maine.gov/revenue/forms/fuel/fueltaxforms.htm
Tax deducted from refund:	No.
Tax paid on separate return:	No.
Difficulty:	Moderate.
File by:	1 year from the date the fuel was purchased.
Attach documents to claim:	None.
Send to address:	Maine Revenue Service P.O. Box 1064 Augusta, ME 04332-1064
Don't file if:	N/A.
State statute(s) supporting refund:	36 §3204-A.
Keep records on file:	6 years.

MARYLAND

Maryland Fuel Tax Refund Claim Instructions: Fuel tax refund for fuel purchased for boats, construction equipment, non-profit-owned equipment, excavating, exports, farming equipment, golf course equipment, hospital vehicles, logging, landfills, lawn equipment, manufacturing, nurseries, off-road use, planes, public utilities, reefer trailers, sand and gravel companies, stationary equipment, government-owned equipment and volunteer fire departments.

INSTRUCTIONS	
State the fuel is purchased in:	MD
Fuel type:	Gasoline, jet fuel and undyed diesel fuel.
Refund type:	Commercial boats, construction equipment, excavating, exports, farming, golf course equipment, hospital vehicles, logging, landfills, lawn equipment, manufacturing, nurseries, off-road use, planes, public utilities, refrigeration (reefer) trailers, sand and gravel companies, stationary equipment, state or Federal government agencies and volunteer fire departments. Other: Vehicles used by non-profits providing transportation services for elderly, handicapped, or low income individuals.
Form name:	Various, see below.
Form #:	Required form(s): **GTD-106**, Motor Fuel Tax – Refund Claim. **COM/RAD-028,** Questionnaire on initial claim. Additional forms required based on refund type: **GT-101-AV**, Aviation. **COM/RAD-061**, Record of Motor Fuel Used. **COM/RAD-079,** Monthly motor fuel activity. **COM/RAD 080**, Export Detail by customer. **COM/RAD 081**, Exports. **COM/RAD-091**, Federal or State Government.
Obtain required forms from:	http://compnet.comp.state.md.us
Tax deducted from refund:	No.
Tax paid on separate return:	No.
Difficulty:	Difficult.
File by:	1 year from the date the fuel was purchased.
Attach documents to claim:	All refund claims must be supported by original invoices. If you submit copies of the original invoices, you must also include a statement that the originals are available.
Send to address:	Comptroller of Maryland Revenue Administration Division Annapolis, MD 21411-0001
Don't file if:	N/A.
State statute(s) supporting refund:	Various.
Keep records on file:	3 years.

Maryland Fuel Tax Refund Claim Instructions: Fuel tax refund for fuel purchased for PTO vehicles.

INSTRUCTIONS	
State the fuel is purchased in:	MD
Fuel type:	Gasoline and undyed diesel fuel.
Refund type:	PTO (power take-off) vehicles. Specific Types: Motor fuel delivery vehicles, concrete mixing/concrete pumping vehicles, solid waste compacting vehicles, qualifying farm equipment vehicles and well-drilling vehicles.
Form name:	Various, see below.
Form #:	Required form(s): **GTD-106PTO**, PTO Refund Claim Form. **COM/RAD-028**, Questionnaire on initial claim. **MFT-049**, Dealer/Seller Schedule of Receipts. **MFT-048**, Dealer/Seller Schedule of Disbursements.
Obtain required forms from:	http://compnet.comp.state.md.us
Tax deducted from refund:	No.
Tax paid on separate return:	No.
Difficulty:	Difficult.
File by:	1 year from the date the fuel was purchased.
Attach documents to claim:	All refund claims must be supported by original invoices. If you submit copies of the original invoices, you must also include a statement that the originals are available for audit purposes.
Send to address:	Comptroller of Maryland Revenue Administration Division Annapolis, MD 21411-0001
Don't file if:	N/A.
State statute(s) supporting refund:	Various.
Keep records on file:	3 years.

MASSACHUSETTS

Massachusetts Fuel Tax Refund Claim Instructions: Fuel tax refund for gasoline purchased for off-road use.

INSTRUCTIONS	
State the fuel is purchased in:	MA
Fuel type:	Gasoline.
Refund type:	Off-road use.
Form name:	*Gasoline Refund Application.*
Form #:	**GT-9.**
Obtain required forms from:	http://www.mass.gov/dor/forms/miscellaneous/fuel-excise/
Tax deducted from refund:	Yes.
Tax paid on separate return:	No.
Difficulty:	Moderate.
File by:	2 years from the date the fuel was purchased.
Attach documents to claim:	Original motor fuel receipts or invoices. All International Fuel Tax Agreement (IFTA) motor carrier licensees are required to remit copies of their quarterly IFTA reports for the period associated with the refund application.
Send to address:	Massachusetts Department of Revenue P.O. Box 7012 Boston, MA 02204
Don't file if:	Sales tax is greater than refund.
State statute(s) supporting refund:	§ 9-64A -7.
Keep records on file:	3 years.

Massachusetts Fuel Tax Refund Claim Instructions: Fuel tax refund for gasoline purchased for farming equipment.

INSTRUCTIONS	
State the fuel is purchased in:	MA
Fuel type:	Gasoline.
Refund type:	Farming equipment.
Form name:	*Gasoline Refund Application for Those Engaged in the Business of Farming.*
Form #:	**GT-9A**.
Obtain required forms from:	http://www.mass.gov/dor/forms/miscellaneous/fuel-excise/
Tax deducted from refund:	Yes.
Tax paid on separate return:	No.
Difficulty:	Moderate.
File by:	Claims for refund of tax based on gasoline used during the taxable year must be filed on or before the 15th day of the fourth month following the close of such taxable year. If the taxable year and calendar year coincide, the application must be filed on or before April 15.
Attach documents to claim:	Original motor fuel receipts or invoices.
Send to address:	Massachusetts Department of Revenue P.O. Box 7012 Boston, MA 02204
Don't file if:	Sales tax is greater than refund.
State statute(s) supporting refund:	§ 9-64A -7a.
Keep records on file:	3 years.

Massachusetts Fuel Tax Refund Claim Instructions: Fuel tax refund for gasoline purchased and used in non-commercial boating and commercial fishing.

INSTRUCTIONS	
State the fuel is purchased in:	MA
Fuel type:	Gasoline.
Refund type:	Non-commercial boating and commercial fishing.
Form name:	*Gasoline Tax Refund Application, Watercraft Use.*
Form #:	**GT-9M.**
Obtain required forms from:	http://www.mass.gov/dor/forms/miscellaneous/fuel-excise/
Tax deducted from refund:	Yes.
Tax paid on separate return:	No.
Difficulty:	Moderate.
File by:	6 months from the date the fuel was purchased.
Attach documents to claim:	Original motor fuel receipts or invoices.
Send to address:	Massachusetts Department of Revenue P.O. Box 7012 Boston, MA 02204
Don't file if:	Sales tax is greater than refund.
State statute(s) supporting refund:	§ 9-64A-7.
Keep records on file:	3 years.

<u>Massachusetts Fuel Tax Refund Claim Instructions</u>: Fuel tax refund for undyed diesel purchased for off-road use.

INSTRUCTIONS	
State the fuel is purchased in:	MA
Fuel type:	Undyed diesel fuel.
Refund type:	Purchasers of off-road use.
Form name:	*Special Fuels Refund Application*.
Form #:	**SFT-9**.
Obtain required forms from:	http://www.mass.gov/dor/forms/miscellaneous/fuel-excise/
Tax deducted from refund:	Yes.
Tax paid on separate return:	No.
Difficulty:	Moderate.
File by:	2 years from the date the fuel was purchased.
Attach documents to claim:	Original motor fuel receipts or invoices.
Send to address:	Massachusetts Department of Revenue P.O. Box 7012 Boston, MA 02204
Don't file if:	Sales tax is greater than refund.
State statute(s) supporting refund:	§ 9-64A-7.
Keep records on file:	3 years.

<u>Massachusetts Fuel Tax Refund Claim Instructions</u>: Fuel tax refund for undyed diesel used on the turnpike.

INSTRUCTIONS	
State the fuel is purchased in:	MA
Fuel type:	Undyed diesel fuel.
Refund type:	Purchasers of fuel used within three preceding days of turnpike use. Applicants having storage facilities must transfer fuel into vehicle tank on day of use or within three preceding days of turnpike use.
Form name:	*Special Fuels Refund Application (Mass. Turnpike Use, Special Fuels Excise).*
Form #:	**SFT-9T**.
Obtain required forms from:	http://www.mass.gov/dor/forms/miscellaneous/fuel-excise/
Tax deducted from refund:	Yes.
Tax paid on separate return:	No.
Difficulty:	Moderate.
File by:	2 years from the date the fuel was purchased.
Attach documents to claim:	Original motor fuel receipts or invoices.
Send to address:	Massachusetts Department of Revenue P.O. Box 7012 Boston, MA 02204
Don't file if:	Sales tax is greater than refund.
State statute(s) supporting refund:	§ 9-64A-7.
Keep records on file:	3 years.

<u>Massachusetts Fuel Tax Refund Claim Instructions</u>: Fuel tax refund for aviation fuel purchased for planes.

INSTRUCTIONS	
State the fuel is purchased in:	MA
Fuel type:	Aviation fuel.
Refund type:	Planes.
Form name:	*Aircraft (Jet) Fuel Refund Application.*
Form #:	**JFT-9**.
Obtain required forms from:	http://www.mass.gov/dor/forms/miscellaneous/fuel-excise/
Tax deducted from refund:	Yes.
Tax paid on separate return:	No.
Difficulty:	Moderate.
File by:	2 years from the date the fuel was purchased.
Attach documents to claim:	Original motor fuel receipts or invoices.
Send to address:	Massachusetts Department of Revenue P.O. Box 7012 Boston, MA 02204
Don't file if:	Sales tax is greater than refund.
State statute(s) supporting refund:	N/A.
Keep records on file:	3 years.

MICHIGAN

Michigan Fuel Tax Refund Claim Instructions: Fuel tax refund for fuel purchased for government-owned vehicles, mass transit buses, planes, racing vehicles, off-road use, PTO vehicles and school buses. Further refund application exists for fuel lost through contamination and fuel exports.

INSTRUCTIONS	
State the fuel is purchased in:	MI
Fuel type:	Gasoline, jet fuel and undyed diesel fuel.
Refund type:	Buses, community action agency vehicles, contamination, fuel loss, exports, racing vehicles, off-road use, planes, PTO (power take-off) equipment, school buses and state and Federal government agencies.
Form name:	Various.
Form #:	Various.
Obtain required forms from:	Call DOR and provide a valid mailing address.
Tax deducted from refund:	No.
Tax paid on separate return:	No.
Difficulty:	Easy.
File by:	The refund claim for gasoline and diesel fuel taxes must be filed within 18 months of the date of purchase of the fuel. The refund claim for aviation fuel or marine fuel must be filed within 6 months of the date of purchase of the fuel.
Attach documents to claim:	Copies of receipts or invoices must be filed with the claim form.
Send to address:	Michigan Department of Treasury Lansing, Michigan 48922
Don't file if:	N/A.
State statute(s) supporting refund:	§ 207-1045 (PTO). § 207-1043 (Stored motor fuel exported by transport truck). § 207-1042 (Motor bus). § 207-1041 (Community Action Agency Vehicle). § 207-1040 (Contaminated, lost, or destroyed fuel). § 207-1039 (Leaded racing fuel or husbandry). § 207-1036 (Licensed exporter). § 207-1035 (School bus owned). § 207-1034 (Government use). § 207-1033 (Off-road use). § 207-1030 (Tax exemption).
Keep records on file:	4 years.

MINNESOTA

Minnesota Fuel Tax Refund Claim Instructions: Fuel tax refund for fuel purchased for airline ground use, biodiesel sales, construction equipment, farming equipment, kerosene, lawn equipment, logging, planes, PTO vehicles, reefer trailers, snowmobiles and well drilling equipment.

INSTRUCTIONS	
State the fuel is purchased in:	MN
Fuel type:	Gasoline, undyed diesel fuel and undyed kerosene.
Refund type:	Airline ground use, biodiesel usage, construction equipment, farming equipment, kerosene, lawn equipment, logging, refrigeration (reefer) trailers, PTO (power take-off) equipment, snowmobiles and well drilling.
Form name:	*Minnesota Motor Fuel Claim for Refund.*
Form #:	**PDR-1.**
Obtain required forms from:	http://taxes.state.mn.us/pages/current_forms.aspx#forms
Tax deducted from refund:	Yes, the fuel on which the motor fuel tax has been refunded is subject to Minnesota sales and use tax, unless specifically exempted by law (i.e. fuel delivered to residential customers for residential heating or fuel used or consumed in agricultural or industrial production).
Tax paid on separate return:	Yes, sales tax must be paid on Minnesota *Sales and Use Tax* Return.
Difficulty:	Difficult.
File by:	Claims must be filed within 1 year and 2 months (425 days) from the date of purchase. The postmark date is considered the filing date. Each claim must cover only one month. Only one claim per period is allowed and if corrections to the original claim are necessary, an amended claim must be filed.
Attach documents to claim:	Copies of motor fuel invoices and receipts not required with claim. If filing for a PTO (power take-off equipment) refund, file **Schedule PDR-1PTO**. Attach a detailed list of all qualifying vehicles for all other refunds involving vehicles or equipment.
Send to address:	Minnesota Revenue Petroleum Taxes Mail Station 3333 St. Paul, MN 55146
Don't file if:	Sales tax is greater than refund.
State statute(s) supporting refund:	M. S. 297A.68, Subd. 19.
Keep records on file:	3½ years.

MISSOURI

Missouri Fuel Tax Refund Claim Instructions: Fuel tax refund for fuel purchased for ATV's, mass transit buses, farming equipment, heating, lawn equipment, off-road use, planes, PTO vehicles, reefer trailers, stationary equipment and government-owned vehicles.

INSTRUCTIONS	
State the fuel is purchased in:	MO
Fuel type:	Gasoline, kerosene and undyed diesel fuel.
Refund type:	ATVs (all-terrain vehicles), buses / mass transit, farming equipment, heating, lawn equipment, off-road use, planes, PTO (power take-off) vehicles, refrigeration (reefer) trailers, stationary equipment, state or Federal government agencies. Other: fuel used as an ingredient or component part of the finished product.
Form name:	Various, see below.
Form #:	Required form(s): **4923**, *Motor Fuel Refund Claim.* **4924**, *Motor Fuel Refund Application. For your first claim.* Additional forms required based on refund type: **588A,** *Schedule C for PTO Equipment.* **4925**, *Marine Fuel Purchases Schedule.*
Obtain required forms from:	http://dor.mo.gov/forms/index.php?category=18
Tax deducted from refund:	Yes (Calculated by Missouri Department of Revenue).
Tax paid on separate return:	No.
Difficulty:	Difficult.
File by:	1 year from the date of purchase or April 15 following the year of the purchase whichever is later.
Attach documents to claim:	Original motor fuel receipts or invoices. The invoices must be marked paid by the seller and contain the date of sale, name and address of the purchaser and seller, number of gallons purchased and price per gallon, Missouri fuel tax and sales tax, if applicable, as separate items.
Send to address:	Missouri Department of Revenue Taxation Division P.O. Box 800 Jefferson City, MO 65105
Don't file if:	Sales tax is greater than refund.
State statute(s) supporting refund:	10-142.815-24.
Keep records on file:	3 years.

MONTANA

<u>Montana Fuel Tax Refund Claim Instructions</u>: Fuel tax refund for fuel purchased for construction equipment, fabrication, golf course equipment, logging, off-road use, oilfield equipment, stationary equipment and trains.

INSTRUCTIONS	
State the fuel is purchased in:	MT
Fuel type:	Gasoline, gasohol and undyed diesel.
Refund type:	Construction equipment (off-road refund), fabrication (off-road refund), golf course equipment (off-road refund), logging (of-road refund), off-road use, oilfield equipment (off-road refund), stationary equipment and trains (off-road refund).
Form name:	*Off-Road Refund Application.*
Form #:	No Form No.
Obtain required forms from:	http://www.mdt.mt.gov/publications/forms.shtml#fuel
Tax deducted from refund:	No.
Tax paid on separate return:	No.
Difficulty:	Moderate.
File by:	3 years from the date the fuel was purchased.
Attach documents to claim:	Original motor fuel receipts or invoices.
Send to address:	Montana Department of Revenue P.O. Box 8019 Helena, MT 59604-8019
Don't file if:	N/A.
State statute(s) supporting refund:	§ 15-70-221, 15-70-356.
Keep records on file:	3 years.

Montana Fuel Tax Refund Claim Instructions: Fuel tax refund for fuel purchased for farming equipment.

INSTRUCTIONS	
State the fuel is purchased in:	MT
Fuel type:	Gasoline, gasohol and undyed diesel.
Refund type:	Farming equipment. Note: Primary source of income (at least 30 percent) must be from agriculture activities – those operations directly associated with farming and ranching.
Form name:	*Agricultural Standard Refund Application.*
Form #:	**MF-27A.**
Obtain required forms from:	http://www.mdt.mt.gov/publications/forms.shtml#fuel
Tax deducted from refund:	No.
Tax paid on separate return:	No.
Difficulty:	Difficult.
File by:	3 years from the date the fuel was purchased.
Attach documents to claim:	Original motor fuel receipts or invoices.
Send to address:	Montana Department of Revenue P.O. Box 8019 Helena, MT 59604-8019
Don't file if:	Percent of gross earned agricultural income is less than 30%.
State statute(s) supporting refund:	§ 15-70-223, 15-70-362.
Keep records on file:	3 years.

<u>Montana Fuel Tax Refund Claim Instructions</u>: Fuel tax refund for undyed diesel purchased for heating purposes.

INSTRUCTIONS	
State the fuel is purchased in:	MT
Fuel type:	Undyed diesel.
Refund type:	Heating.
Form name:	Various, see below.
Form #:	Required form(s): **MF-27G**, *Application for Refund of Heating Fuel Tax.* **Schedule 3**, *Invoice Schedule.*
Obtain required forms from:	http://www.mdt.mt.gov/publications/forms.shtml#fuel
Tax deducted from refund:	No.
Tax paid on separate return:	No.
Difficulty:	Easy.
File by:	3 years from the date the fuel was purchased.
Attach documents to claim:	Original motor fuel receipts or invoices.
Send to address:	Montana Department of Revenue P.O. Box 8019 Helena, MT 59604-8019
Don't file if:	N/A.
State statute(s) supporting refund:	§ 15-70-221, 15-70-356.
Keep records on file:	3 years.

<u>Montana Fuel Tax Refund Claim Instructions</u>: Fuel tax refund for undyed diesel purchased for reefer trailers.

INSTRUCTIONS	
State the fuel is purchased in:	MT
Fuel type:	Undyed diesel.
Refund type:	Refrigeration (reefer) trailers.
Form name:	*Refrigerator Fuel Refund Application.*
Form #:	**MF-93.**
Obtain required forms from:	http://www.mdt.mt.gov/publications/forms.shtml#fuel
Tax deducted from refund:	No.
Tax paid on separate return:	No.
Difficulty:	Easy.
File by:	3 years from the date the fuel was purchased.
Attach documents to claim:	Original motor fuel receipts or invoices.
Send to address:	Montana Department of Revenue P.O. Box 8019 Helena, MT 59604-8019
Don't file if:	N/A.
State statute(s) supporting refund:	§ 15-70-221, 15-70-356.
Keep records on file:	3 years.

Montana Fuel Tax Refund Claim Instructions: Fuel tax refund for undyed diesel purchased for fire trucks, school buses and government-owned vehicles.

INSTRUCTIONS	
State the fuel is purchased in:	MT
Fuel type:	Undyed diesel.
Refund type:	Fire Departments, school buses, state and Federal government agencies. Note: No refund is allowed for buses under contract.
Form name:	*Form for Federal, State, Local Governments and School Districts.*
Form #:	**MF-27G**.
Obtain required forms from:	http://www.mdt.mt.gov/publications/forms.shtml#fuel
Tax deducted from refund:	No.
Tax paid on separate return:	No.
Difficulty:	Easy.
File by:	3 years from the date the fuel was purchased.
Attach documents to claim:	Original motor fuel receipts or invoices.
Send to address:	Montana Department of Revenue P.O. Box 8019 Helena, MT 59604-8019
Don't file if:	N/A.
State statute(s) supporting refund:	§ 15-70-221, 15-70-356.
Keep records on file:	3 years.

Montana Fuel Tax Refund Claim Instructions: Fuel tax refund for fuel purchased for PTO vehicles.

INSTRUCTIONS	
State the fuel is purchased in:	MT
Fuel type:	Gasoline, gasohol and undyed diesel fuel.
Refund type:	PTO (power take-off) vehicles. Note: Climate control functions are not considered PTO (Power Take off).
Form name:	*PTO Refund Application.*
Form #:	**MF-27P**.
Obtain required forms from:	http://www.mdt.mt.gov/publications/forms.shtml#fuel
Tax deducted from refund:	No.
Tax paid on separate return:	No.
Difficulty:	Moderate.
File by:	3 years from the date the fuel was purchased.
Attach documents to claim:	Original motor fuel receipts or invoices.
Send to address:	Montana Department of Revenue P.O. Box 8019 Helena, MT 59604-8019
Don't file if:	N/A.
State statute(s) supporting refund:	§ 15-70-221, 15-70-356.
Keep records on file:	3 years.

Montana Fuel Tax Refund Claim Instructions: Fuel tax refund for biodiesel sold by distributors and retailers.

INSTRUCTIONS	
State the fuel is purchased in:	MT
Fuel type:	Biodiesel fuel.
Refund type:	Distributors and retailers of biodiesel fuel.
Form name:	*Biodiesel Fuel Tax Application.*
Form #:	No Form No.
Obtain required forms from:	http://www.mdt.mt.gov/publications/forms.shtml#fuel
Tax deducted from refund:	No.
Tax paid on separate return:	No.
Difficulty:	Moderate.
File by:	30 days at the end of each calendar quarter.
Attach documents to claim:	Original motor fuel receipts or invoices.
Send to address:	Fuel Tax Management and Analysis Bureau (FTMA) Department of Transportation 2701 Prospect Avenue P.O. Box 201001 Helena, MT 59620
Don't file if:	N/A.
State statute(s) supporting refund:	§ 15-70-601.
Keep records on file:	3 years.

<u>Montana Fuel Tax Refund Claim Instructions</u>: Fuel tax refund for producers of biodiesel fuel.

INSTRUCTIONS	
State the fuel is purchased in:	MT
Fuel type:	Biodiesel fuel.
Refund type:	Producers of biodiesel fuel.
Form name:	*Biodiesel producer's tax incentive application.*
Form #:	No Form No.
Obtain required forms from:	http://www.mdt.mt.gov/publications/forms.shtml#fuel
Tax deducted from refund:	No.
Tax paid on separate return:	No.
Difficulty:	Moderate.
File by:	3 years from the date the fuel was purchased.
Attach documents to claim:	Original motor fuel receipts or invoices.
Send to address:	Fuel Tax Management and Analysis Bureau (FTMA) Department of Transportation 2701 Prospect Avenue P.O. Box 201001 Helena, MT 59620
Don't file if:	N/A.
State statute(s) supporting refund:	§ 15-70-601.
Keep records on file:	3 years.

<u>Montana Fuel Tax Return Credit Instructions</u>: Bad debt credit for fuel suppliers.

INSTRUCTIONS	
State the fuel is purchased in:	MT
Fuel type:	Gasoline and undyed diesel.
Refund type:	Bad debt credit for fuel suppliers.
Form name:	*Bad Debt Credit Application for Motor Fuels Tax.*
Form #:	**MF-33.**
Obtain required forms from:	http://www.mdt.mt.gov/publications/forms.shtml#fuel
Tax deducted from refund:	No.
Tax paid on separate return:	No.
Difficulty:	Moderate.
File by:	3 years from the date the fuel was purchased.
Attach documents to claim:	Original motor fuel receipts or invoices. Attach a copy of the *U.S. Corporation Income Tax* Reporting Form (Form **1120**) and write in the time period covered by Form **1120** in Part B.
Send to address:	Fuel Tax Management and Analysis Bureau (FTMA) Department of Transportation 2701 Prospect Avenue P.O. Box 201001 Helena, MT 59620
Don't file if:	Tax credits less than $200.00 or greater for each purchaser (debtor).
State statute(s) supporting refund:	§ 15-70-221, 15-70-356.
Keep records on file:	3 years.

NEBRASKA

Nebraska Fuel Tax Refund Claim Instructions: Fuel tax refund for fuel purchased for government-owned vehicles, planes, reefer trailers and unlicensed equipment. Other refund applications include fuel loss and contamination.

INSTRUCTIONS	
State the fuel is purchased in:	NE
Fuel type:	Aviation gasoline, gasoline, gasohol, ethanol, jet fuel, undyed biodiesel blends and undyed diesel fuel.
Refund type:	Contamination / loss, Federal government agencies, planes, refrigeration (reefer) trailers and unlicensed equipment.
Form name:	*Nebraska Non-Ag Use Motor Fuels Tax Refund Claim.*
Form #:	**Form 84.**
Obtain required forms from:	Yes, on tax paid on diesel fuel used for reefer units or home heating. If you are claiming a refund for tax paid on gasoline or gasohol which was subsequently used to fuel an airplane, the claim must be reduced by the aviation gasoline tax rate of 5¢ per gallon.
Tax deducted from refund:	http://www.dmvnv.com/mcforms.htm
Tax paid on separate return:	No.
Difficulty:	Difficult.
File by:	In most cases, 3 years. Claims filed for refunds for aviation jet fuel or gasoline used in a FAA-approved air school must be filed within 7 months of the date of purchase.
Attach documents to claim:	Copies of motor fuel receipts or invoices. The filer will also need to provide the following: A.) Legible copies of fuel logs. B.) Equipment list.
Send to address:	Motor Fuels Division Nebraska Department of Revenue P.O. Box 98904 Lincoln, NE 68509
Don't file if:	Annual claim is less than $25.00. You may not carry over amounts from one year to another. The Petroleum Release Remedial Action Fee has a $10 minimum per year amount. Fuel used in a licensed motor vehicle is not eligible for a refund regardless of how the vehicle was used. Fuel used in licensed motor vehicles by state and local governmental entities, including school districts, does not qualify for a refund.
State statute(s) supporting refund:	§ 66-726.
Keep records on file:	3 years.

NEVADA

<u>Nevada Fuel Tax Refund Claim Instructions</u>: Fuel tax refund for motor fuel purchased for commercial boating, commercial snowmobiles, construction equipment, farming, golf course equipment, lawn equipment, logging, off-road vehicle usage, oilfield equipment, planes and stationary equipment.

INSTRUCTIONS	
State the fuel is purchased in:	NV
Fuel type:	E85, gasoline and gasohol.
Refund type:	Aviation, commercial marine usage, commercial snowmobile usage, construction equipment, farming equipment, golf course equipment, lawn equipment, logging, mining, off-road use, oilfield equipment and stationary equipment.
Form name:	*Gasoline Tax Refund Request.*
Form #:	**MC45-G.**
Obtain required forms from:	http://www.dmvnv.com/pdfforms/mc045g.pdf
Tax deducted from refund:	No.
Tax paid on separate return:	No.
Difficulty:	Moderate.
File by:	1 year from the date the fuel was purchased.
Attach documents to claim:	Original motor fuel receipts, invoices, bulk tank fuel logs, tank truck fuel logs, and equipment lists, as applicable.
Send to address:	Nevada Department of Revenue Motor Carrier Division 555 Wright Wy. Carson City, NV 89711
Don't file if:	Claim is for less than 200 gallons.
State statute(s) supporting refund:	NRS § 366.650.
Keep records on file:	4 years.

<u>Nevada Fuel Tax Refund Claim Instructions</u>: Fuel tax refund for fuel purchased for commercial boating, construction equipment, farming, fire trucks, golf course equipment, heating, logging, mining, off-road use, oilfield equipment, PTO vehicles, public utilities, reefer trailers, school buses, stationary equipment and government-owned vehicles.

INSTRUCTIONS	
State the fuel is purchased in:	NV
Fuel type:	Biodiesel, CNG (compressed natural gas), LPG (liquefied petroleum gas), kerosene, and undyed diesel fuel.
Refund type:	Commercial boating, commercial snowmobiles, construction equipment, fabrication, farming equipment, fire trucks, golf course equipment, heating, logging, mining, off-road use, oilfield equipment, PTO (power take-off) vehicles, public utilities, refrigeration (reefer) trailers, school buses, stationary equipment, and state and Federal government agencies.
Form name:	*Fuel Tax Refund Request Form.*
Form #:	http://www.dmvnv.com/mcforms.htm
Obtain required forms from:	**MC45.**
Tax deducted from refund:	No.
Tax paid on separate return:	No.
Difficulty:	Moderate.
File by:	1 year from the date the fuel was purchased.
Attach documents to claim:	Original motor fuel receipts, invoices, fuel usage logs, mileage logs, bulk tank inventory readings (if applicable).
Send to address:	Nevada Department of Revenue Motor Carrier Division 555 Wright Wy. Carson City, NV 89711
Don't file if:	Claim is less than 200 gallons.
State statute(s) supporting refund:	NRS § 366.650.
Keep records on file:	4 years.

NEW HAMPSHIRE

<u>New Hampshire Fuel Tax Refund Claim Instructions</u>: Road toll fee refund for licensed distributors of fuel.

INSTRUCTIONS	
State the fuel is purchased in:	NH
Fuel type:	Gasoline and undyed diesel fuel.
Refund type:	3/4 refund of tax paid on fuel sold by retail detailer on behalf of licensed distributor.
Form name:	*Road Toll Refund Application - Retail Dealer.*
Form #:	**RT-115.**
Obtain required forms from:	http://www.nh.gov/safety/divisions/administration/roadtoll/forms.html
Tax deducted from refund:	No.
Tax paid on separate return:	No.
Difficulty:	Easy.
File by:	90 days after each 6 month period ending June 30th and Dec 31st.
Attach documents to claim:	All applications must be accompanied by a statement from a licensed NH fuel distributor for gross purchases of motor fuel made by the retail dealer during the six month period. Keep mileage logs, fuel receipts, and bus route logs on hand for auditing purposes. Attach RT115 Schedule of Sales To NH Retail Dealers completed by distributor.
Send to address:	State of New Hampshire Department of Safety Division of Administration Road Toll Bureau 33 Hazen Dr. Concord, NH 03305
Don't file if:	N/A.
State statute(s) supporting refund:	§ 21-260-47.
Keep records on file:	4 years.

New Hampshire Fuel Tax Refund Claim Instructions: Fuel tax refund for undyed diesel fuel purchased for off-road use.

INSTRUCTIONS	
State the fuel is purchased in:	NH
Fuel type:	Undyed diesel fuel.
Refund type:	Off-road use. Note: The road toll must have been paid on this fuel.
Form name:	*Road Toll Refund Application - Toll Paid On Special Fuel Only.*
Form #:	**RT-122D.**
Obtain required forms from:	http://www.nh.gov/safety/divisions/administration/roadtoll/forms.html
Tax deducted from refund:	No.
Tax paid on separate return:	No.
Difficulty:	Moderate.
File by:	April 15 following the year of purchase for an annual claim.
Attach documents to claim:	Copies of receipts or invoices must be filed with the claim form of all purchases bearing name and address of supplier and name of the applicant together with evidence of payment must be attached. Evidence of payment-each invoice must be receipted by the supplier as being paid or if payment is made by check, date of payment together with check number must appear on the invoice. Evidence of erasures or changes in either dates or amounts shown on invoices or evidence of payment shall result in the invoices being disallowed. Invoices cannot be returned.
Send to address:	State of New Hampshire Department of Safety Division of Administration Road Toll Bureau 33 Hazen Dr. Concord, NH 03305
Don't file if:	Claim is for less than $10.00.
State statute(s) supporting refund:	§ 21-260-47.
Keep records on file:	4 years.

New Hampshire Fuel Tax Refund Claim Instructions: Fuel tax refund for gasoline purchased for off-road use.

INSTRUCTIONS	
State the fuel is purchased in:	NH
Fuel type:	Gasoline.
Refund type:	Off-road use.
Form name:	*Road Toll Refund Application - Gasoline Only.*
Form #:	**RT-122G.**
Obtain required forms from:	http://www.nh.gov/safety/divisions/administration/roadtoll/forms.html
Tax deducted from refund:	No.
Tax paid on separate return:	No.
Difficulty:	Moderate.
File by:	April 15 following the year of purchase for an annual claim.
Attach documents to claim:	Copies of receipts or invoices must be filed with the claim form of all purchases bearing name and address of supplier and name of the applicant together with evidence of payment must be attached. Evidence of payment-each invoice must be receipted by the supplier as being paid or if payment is made by check, date of payment together with check number must appear on the invoice. Evidence of erasures or changes in either dates or amounts shown on invoices or evidence of payment shall result in the invoices being disallowed. Invoices cannot be returned.
Send to address:	State of New Hampshire Department of Safety Division of Administration Road Toll Bureau 33 Hazen Dr. Concord, NH 03305
Don't file if:	Claim is for less than $10.00.
State statute(s) supporting refund:	§ 21-260-47.
Keep records on file:	4 years.

New Hampshire Fuel Tax Refund Claim Instructions: Fuel tax refund for gasoline purchased for boats and snowmobiles.

INSTRUCTIONS	
State the fuel is purchased in:	NH
Fuel type:	Gasoline.
Refund type:	Boats and snowmobiles.
Form name:	*Road Toll Refund Application Off Highway Recreational Vehicles, Snowmobiles, and Boats.*
Form #:	**RT-123**.
Obtain required forms from:	http://www.nh.gov/safety/divisions/administration/roadtoll/forms.html
Tax deducted from refund:	No.
Tax paid on separate return:	No.
Difficulty:	Moderate.
File by:	April 15 following the year of purchase for an annual claim.
Attach documents to claim:	Original receipts or invoices must be filed with the claim form of all purchases bearing name and address of supplier and name of the applicant together with evidence of payment must be attached. Evidence of payment-each invoice must be receipted by the supplier as being paid or if payment is made by check, date of payment together with check number must appear on the invoice. Evidence of erasures or changes in either dates or amounts shown on invoices or evidence of payment shall result in the invoices being disallowed. Invoices cannot be returned.
Send to address:	State of New Hampshire Department of Safety Division of Administration Road Toll Bureau 33 Hazen Dr. Concord, NH 03305
Don't file if:	Claim is for less than $10.00.
State statute(s) supporting refund:	§ 21-260-47.
Keep records on file:	4 years.

<u>New Hampshire Fuel Tax Refund Claim Instructions</u>: Fuel tax refund by purchasers of diesel fuel for government-owned vehicles and equipment.

INSTRUCTIONS	
State the fuel is purchased in:	NH
Fuel type:	Undyed diesel fuel.
Refund type:	Municipal and county government agencies.
Form name:	*Refund Application Municipal and County – Tax Paid Diesel Only.*
Form #:	**RT 125 D.**
Obtain required forms from:	http://www.nh.gov/safety/divisions/administration/roadtoll/forms.html
Tax deducted from refund:	No.
Tax paid on separate return:	No.
Difficulty:	Moderate.
File by:	April 15 following the year of purchase for an annual claim.
Attach documents to claim:	Original receipts or invoices must be filed with the claim form of all purchases bearing name and address of supplier and name of the applicant together with evidence of payment must be attached. Evidence of payment-each invoice must be receipted by the supplier as being paid or if payment is made by check, date of payment together with check number must appear on the invoice. Evidence of erasures or changes in either dates or amounts shown on invoices or evidence of payment shall result in the invoices being disallowed. Invoices cannot be returned.
Send to address:	State of New Hampshire Department of Safety Division of Administration Road Toll Bureau 33 Hazen Dr. Concord, NH 03305
Don't file if:	Claim is for less than $10.00.
State statute(s) supporting refund:	§ 21-260-47.
Keep records on file:	4 years.

New Hampshire Fuel Tax Refund Claim Instructions: Fuel tax refund for gasoline purchased for government-owned vehicles and equipment.

INSTRUCTIONS	
State the fuel is purchased in:	NH
Fuel type:	Gasoline.
Refund type:	Municipal and county government.
Form name:	*Refund Application Municipal and County – Gasoline Only.*
Form #:	**RT 125 G.**
Obtain required forms from:	http://www.nh.gov/safety/divisions/administration/roadtoll/forms.html
Tax deducted from refund:	No.
Tax paid on separate return:	No.
Difficulty:	Moderate.
File by:	April 15 following the year of purchase for an annual claim.
Attach documents to claim:	Original receipts or invoices must be filed with the claim form of all purchases bearing name and address of supplier and name of the applicant together with evidence of payment must be attached. Evidence of payment-each invoice must be receipted by the supplier as being paid or if payment is made by check, date of payment together with check number must appear on the invoice. Evidence of erasures or changes in either dates or amounts shown on invoices or evidence of payment shall result in the invoices being disallowed.
Send to address:	State of New Hampshire Department of Safety Division of Administration Road Toll Bureau 33 Hazen Dr. Concord, NH 03305
Don't file if:	Claim is for less than $10.00.
State statute(s) supporting refund:	§ 21-260-47.
Keep records on file:	4 years.

New Hampshire Fuel Tax Refund Claim Instructions: Fuel tax refund of fuel purchased for farming equipment.

INSTRUCTIONS	
State the fuel is purchased in:	NH
Fuel type:	Gasoline and undyed diesel fuel.
Refund type:	Farming equipment.
Form name:	*Road Toll Refund Application Farm Use Only.*
Form #:	**RT 126.**
Obtain required forms from:	http://www.nh.gov/safety/divisions/administration/roadtoll/forms.html
Tax deducted from refund:	No.
Tax paid on separate return:	No.
Difficulty:	Moderate.
File by:	April 15 following the year of purchase for an annual claim.
Attach documents to claim:	Copies of receipts or invoices must be filed with the claim form of all purchases bearing name and address of supplier and name of the applicant together with evidence of payment must be attached. Evidence of payment-each invoice must be receipted by the supplier as being paid or if payment is made by check, date of payment together with check number must appear on the invoice. Evidence of erasures or changes in either dates or amounts shown on invoices or evidence of payment shall result in the invoices being disallowed.
Send to address:	State of New Hampshire Department of Safety Division of Administration Road Toll Bureau 33 Hazen Dr. Concord, NH 03305
Don't file if:	Claim is for less than $750.00.
State statute(s) supporting refund:	§ 21-260-47.
Keep records on file:	4 years.

New Hampshire Fuel Tax Refund Claim Instructions: Fuel tax refund for purchasers of undyed diesel fuel for school buses.

INSTRUCTIONS	
State the fuel is purchased in:	NH
Fuel type:	Undyed diesel fuel.
Refund type:	School buses.
Form name:	*Refund Application – Private School Bus Owner – Tax Paid Diesel Only.*
Form #:	**RT 127 D.**
Obtain required forms from:	http://www.nh.gov/safety/divisions/administration/roadtoll/forms.html
Tax deducted from refund:	No.
Tax paid on separate return:	No.
Difficulty:	Moderate.
File by:	April 15 following the year of purchase for an annual claim.
Attach documents to claim:	Original receipts or invoices, bearing the name and address of the supplier and the name of the applicant, date of purchase and gallons together with evidence of payment must be attached. Invoices cannot be returned to the applicant. (A spreadsheet or computerized printout with all information of receipt may be submitted.) Note: Each invoice must be receipted by the supplier as being paid, or if payment is made by check, the date of payment and check number must be supplied. Evidence of erasures or changes in either dates or amounts shown on the invoices or evidence of payment shall result in the invoices being disallowed.
Send to address:	State of New Hampshire Department of Safety Division of Administration Road Toll Bureau 33 Hazen Dr. Concord, NH 03305
Don't file if:	Claim is for less than $750.00.
State statute(s) supporting refund:	§ 21-260-47.
Keep records on file:	4 years.

<u>New Hampshire Fuel Tax Refund Claim Instructions</u>: Fuel tax refund for purchasers of motor fuel for school buses.

INSTRUCTIONS	
State the fuel is purchased in:	NH
Fuel type:	Gasoline.
Refund type:	School buses.
Form name:	*Refund Application – Private School Bus Owner – Gasoline Only.*
Form #:	**RT 127 G.**
Obtain required forms from:	http://www.nh.gov/safety/divisions/administration/roadtoll/forms.html
Tax deducted from refund:	No.
Tax paid on separate return:	No.
Difficulty:	Moderate.
File by:	April 15 following the year of purchase for an annual claim.
Attach documents to claim:	Original receipts or invoices, bearing the name and address of the supplier and the name of the applicant, date of purchase and gallons together with evidence of payment must be attached. Invoices cannot be returned to the applicant. (A spreadsheet or computerized printout with all information of receipt may be submitted.) Note: Each invoice must be receipted by the supplier as being paid, or if payment is made by check, the date of payment and check number must be supplied. Evidence of erasures or changes in either dates or amounts shown on the invoices or evidence of payment shall result in the invoices being disallowed.
Send to address:	State of New Hampshire Department of Safety Division of Administration Road Toll Bureau 33 Hazen Dr. Concord, NH 03305
Don't file if:	Claim is for less than $750.00.
State statute(s) supporting refund:	§ 21-260-47.
Keep records on file:	4 years.

NEW JERSEY

New Jersey Fuel Tax Refund Claim Instructions: Fuel tax refund by purchasers of fuel for ambulances, boats, construction equipment, cleaning, fuel exports, farming equipment, fire trucks, heating, mass transit buses, off-road use, reefer trailers, trains and other specialized vehicles.

INSTRUCTIONS	
State the fuel is purchased in:	NJ
Fuel type:	Gasoline and undyed diesel fuel.
Refund type:	Ambulances, aviation, buses, boy scouts, commercial boating, construction equipment, cleaning, exports, farming, fire department, heating, off-road equipment, automobiles less than 5,000 G.V.W., refrigeration (reefer) trailers, rural free delivery carriers, stationary equipment, trains and volunteer first air or rescue squads.
Form name:	Various, see below.
Form #:	Required form(s): **A-3711-MF**, *Motor Fuel Tax Refund Claim.* **Form GR-3**, *Preliminary Refund Questionnaire.*
Obtain required forms from:	http://www.state.nj.us/treasury/taxation/prntmf.shtml
Tax deducted from refund:	No.
Tax paid on separate return:	No.
Difficulty:	Difficult.
File by:	6 months from the date the fuel was purchased but file monthly.
Attach documents to claim:	• Copies of motor fuel receipts or invoices. • *Bus Fuel Tax Refund*: Include terminal points of each route, length of each route, mileage operated in each municipality, number of buses operating on each route. Support statement by a copy of schedules and copy of franchise as approved by Public Utility Commission. • *Rural Delivery Carriers*: Include post office and R.D. number, number of trips daily, mileage each trip. • *Fisherman*: Include the length and beam of each boat. • *Contractors*: Include the capacity of all shovels, dredges and scoops and the tonnage of all licensed and non-licensed trucks.
Send to address:	New Jersey Division of Taxation Motor Fuels Tax Section P.O. Box 243 Trenton, NJ 08695
Don't file if:	Do not include purchases of more than 1 calendar month.
State statute(s) supporting refund:	§ 54-39-112.
Keep records on file:	2 years.

NEW MEXICO

New Mexico Fuel Tax Refund Claim Instructions: Fuel tax refund by purchasers of fuel for planes.

INSTRUCTIONS	
State the fuel is purchased in:	NM
Fuel type:	Aviation gasoline.
Refund type:	Aviation.
Form name:	*Application for Aviation Gas Tax Refund.*
Form #:	Forms provided by New Mexico DOR after filing registration for refund form # **RPD-41173**.
Obtain required forms from:	Call New Mexico DOR.
Tax deducted from refund:	A refund of gasoline tax claimed must be reduced by the compensating tax due on the fuel purchase process.
Tax paid on separate return:	No.
Difficulty:	Moderate.
File by:	6 months of the date the gasoline was purchased and used.
Attach documents to claim:	Original of each receipt / invoice for which the refund claim is based. Include the permit number.
Send to address:	Revenue Processing Division Special Tax Programs & Services P.O. Box 25123 Santa Fe, NM 87504-5123
Don't file if:	Holders of Bulk Storage User Permits Do Not Qualify For This Refund.
State statute(s) supporting refund:	N/A.
Keep records on file:	N/A.

New Mexico Fuel Tax Refund Claim Instructions: Fuel tax refund by purchasers of diesel fuel for off-road use, PTO vehicles and reefer trailers.

INSTRUCTIONS	
State the fuel is purchased in:	NM
Fuel type:	Undyed diesel fuel.
Refund type:	Purchasers of undyed diesel fuel for off-road equipment, reefer trailers, auxiliary equipment by a power take-off from the main engine or transmission of the vehicle, non-automotive apparatus permanently mounted on a vehicle using fuel from the supply tank of the vehicle.
Form name:	N/A.
Form #:	Forms provided by New Mexico DOR after filing registration for refund form **RPD-41226** including a list of equipment being fueled. If a vehicle is registered outside of New Mexico and has an IRP registration, include a copy of state's IRP registration.
Obtain required forms from:	Call New Mexico DOR.
Tax deducted from refund:	No.
Tax paid on separate return:	No.
Difficulty:	Moderate.
File by:	6 months.
Attach documents to claim:	N/A.
Send to address:	Revenue Processing Division Special Tax Programs & Services P.O. Box 25123 Santa Fe, NM 87504-5123
Don't file if:	Holders of bulk storage user permits do not qualify for this refund.
State statute(s) supporting refund:	Various.
Keep records on file:	Indefinitely.

NEW YORK

<u>New York Fuel Tax Refund Claim Instructions</u>: Fuel tax refund for fuel purchased for ambulances, boats, construction, contracting, farming, government-owned vehicles, heating, hospitals, off-road vehicles, planes, reefer trailers, rescue squad equipment, school buses, snowmobiles, trains and other specialized vehicles.

INSTRUCTIONS	
State the fuel is purchased in:	NY
Fuel type:	Gasoline and undyed diesel fuel.
Refund type:	Ambulances, construction, contracting, farming, hospitals, heating, marine, Native American, planes, refrigeration (reefer) trailers, rescue squads, schools, snowmobiles (in snowmobile clubs), state and Federal government agencies, trains and volunteer fire companies.
Form name:	*Motor/Diesel Motor Fuel Tax Refund Application.*
Form #:	**FT-946/1046.**
Obtain required forms from:	http://www.tax.ny.gov/forms/pbt_refund_apps_current.htm
Tax deducted from refund:	No.
Tax paid on separate return:	No.
Difficulty:	Moderate.
File by:	Beginning inventory should not include purchases made more than 2 years prior to date of filing a claim.
Attach documents to claim:	Original invoices or other substantiation as required by all forms and mail all forms in one envelope.
Send to address:	NYS Tax Department Fuel Tax Refund Unit P.O. Box 5501 Albany, NY 12205
Don't file if:	N/A.
State statute(s) supporting refund:	Articles 13-A § 301-b, 13-A § 301-c, 28-3 § 1116.
Keep records on file:	3 years.

New York Fuel Tax Refund Claim Instructions: Petroleum business tax refund for fuel purchased for off-road use.

INSTRUCTIONS	
State the fuel is purchased in:	NY
Fuel type:	Undyed diesel fuel or residual petroleum product.
Refund type:	Petroleum business tax passed through for off-road use and commercial gallonage. Note: This includes fuel that does not qualify for the manufacturing exemption, the not-for-profit organization exemption, or the utility credit. This also does not include sales of non-highway diesel motor fuel or residual petroleum product for nonresidential heating purposes (heating manufacturing facilities, farm buildings, office buildings, stores, churches, hotels or similar structures).
Form name:	*Reimbursement Application for Petroleum Business Tax on Fuel Used for Commercial Gallonage.*
Form #:	**AU-473.**
Obtain required forms from:	http://www.tax.ny.gov/forms/pbt_refund_apps_current.htm
Tax deducted from refund:	No.
Tax paid on separate return:	No.
Difficulty:	Moderate.
File by:	Claims for refund of the petroleum business tax must be filed within 3 years from the date of purchase.
Attach documents to claim:	You must furnish copies of purchase invoices signed by the dealer or monthly statements, showing the name and address of the dealer and purchaser, date of purchase, number of gallons, type of fuel and the motor fuel excise tax, petroleum business tax and sales tax listed separately. Claimants must keep a record of all fuel purchases and the manner in which the fuel was used.
Send to address:	NYS Tax Department Fuel Tax Refund Unit P.O. Box 5501 Albany, NY 12205
Don't file if:	N/A.
State statute(s) supporting refund:	Article 13-A § 301-c.
Keep records on file:	3 years.

<u>New York Fuel Tax Refund Claim Instructions</u>: Fuel tax refund for fuel purchased for government-owned vehicles and equipment.

INSTRUCTIONS	
State the fuel is purchased in:	NY
Fuel type:	Gasoline and undyed diesel fuel paid by the distributor.
Refund type:	State and Federal government agencies. Any person, who is registered with the Department as a Diesel Motor Fuel Distributor and/or a Motor Fuel Distributor, may use this form to claim a refund/reimbursement of the taxes prepaid to their supplier on fuel sold to governmental entities.
Form name:	*Application for Refund/Reimbursement of Taxes Paid on Fuel Sold to Governmental Entities by Registered Distributors.*
Form #:	**AU-629.**
Obtain required forms from:	http://www.tax.ny.gov/forms/pbt_refund_apps_current.htm
Tax deducted from refund:	No.
Tax paid on separate return:	No.
Difficulty:	Easy.
File by:	3 years from the date the fuel was purchased. Claims for refund of the New York State and local sales tax must be filed within three years from the date the tax was due.
Attach documents to claim:	You must furnish proof of tax-free sales in the form of original sales invoices issued to the governmental entity.
Send to address:	NYS Tax Department Fuel Tax Refund Unit P.O. Box 5501 Albany, NY 12205
Don't file if:	N/A.
State statute(s) supporting refund:	Article 13-A § 301-b, 28-3 § 1116.
Keep records on file:	3 years.

New York Fuel Tax Refund Claim Instructions: Petroleum business tax refund for retailers of fuel used in ferries and other exemption organizations.

INSTRUCTIONS	
State the fuel is purchased in:	NY
Fuel type:	Gasoline, undyed diesel, and residual petroleum product paid by retailers, wholesalers, jobbers and other exempt organizations.
Refund type:	Petroleum business tax for motor fuel from fuel sold by retail filing stations, wholesalers and jobbers of motor fuel, ferries and other exempt organizations.
Form name:	*Application for Reimbursement of the Petroleum Business Tax.*
Form #:	**AU-630.**
Obtain required forms from:	http://www.tax.ny.gov/forms/pbt_refund_apps_current.htm
Tax deducted from refund:	No.
Tax paid on separate return:	No.
Difficulty:	Easy.
File by:	3 years from the date the fuel was purchased.
Attach documents to claim:	• Original purchase invoices showing the supplier's name and address, purchaser's name and address, date of purchase, number of gallons, type of fuel purchased, and that the tax was included in the purchase price; or • For purchases of motor fuel, a properly completed Form **FT-935**, *Certification of Taxes Paid on Motor Fuel*, or, for purchases of diesel motor fuel, a properly completed Form **FT-1000**, *Certificate of Prepayment or Payment of Taxes on Diesel Motor Fuel.*
Send to address:	NYS Tax Department Fuel Tax Refund Unit P.O. Box 5501 Albany, NY 12205
Don't file if:	N/A.
State statute(s) supporting refund:	Article 13-A § 301-b, 28-3 § 1116.
Keep records on file:	3 years.

<u>New York Fuel Tax Refund Claim Instructions</u>: Fuel tax refund for fuel purchased for commercial fishing.

INSTRUCTIONS	
State the fuel is purchased in:	NY
Fuel type:	Gasoline and undyed diesel fuel.
Refund type:	Excise tax, petroleum business tax, and sales tax paid on gasoline and undyed diesel fuel.
Form name:	Commercial fishing.
Form #:	**AU-631.**
Obtain required forms from:	http://www.tax.ny.gov/forms/pbt_refund_apps_current.htm
Tax deducted from refund:	No.
Tax paid on separate return:	No.
Difficulty:	Easy.
File by:	3 years from the date the fuel was purchased. Claims for refund of the New York State and local sales tax should be filed within 3 years from the date the tax was due.
Attach documents to claim:	• Copies of invoices showing each tax (motor fuel and/or diesel motor fuel excise tax, petroleum business tax, and sales tax) listed separately, and • United States Coast Guard documentation (copy), if the watercraft is required to be documented, and • Federal Fisheries Permit (copy) and/or current license issued by the New York State Department of Environmental Conservation with filer's first claim.
Send to address:	NYS Tax Department Fuel Tax Refund Unit P.O. Box 5501 Albany, NY 12205
Don't file if:	N/A.
State statute(s) supporting refund:	Article 13-A § 301-b, 28-3 § 1116.
Keep records on file:	3 years.

New York Fuel Tax Refund Claim Instructions: Petroleum business tax refund for retailers of fuel sold to customers where the amount due is uncollected as bad debt.

INSTRUCTIONS	
State the fuel is purchased in:	NY
Fuel type:	Gasoline, gasohol, undyed diesel fuel, kerosene, jet fuel, residual petroleum product and propane.
Refund type:	Bad debt. Note: To claim a refund of tax paid on a debt written off, the petroleum business or aviation fuel business must have paid the imposed tax to the Tax Department on its return.
Form name:	*Application for Refund of the Petroleum Business Tax Because of a Bad Debt.*
Form #:	**AU-474.**
Obtain required forms from:	http://www.tax.ny.gov/forms/pbt_refund_apps_current.htm
Tax deducted from refund:	No.
Tax paid on separate return:	No, however, to claim a refund of tax paid on a debt written off, the petroleum business or aviation fuel business must have paid the imposed tax to the Tax Department on its return.
Difficulty:	Moderate.
File by:	3 years from the time that the debt was written off and deducted as a worthless debt for Federal income tax purposes.
Attach documents to claim:	None.
Send to address:	NYS Tax Department Fuel Tax Refund Unit P.O. Box 5501 Albany, NY 12205
Don't file if:	N/A.
State statute(s) supporting refund:	Article 13-A § 301-I.
Keep records on file:	3 years.

New York Fuel Tax Refund Claim Instructions: Petroleum business tax refund for fuel purchased for omnibus carriers and nonpublic school operators.

INSTRUCTIONS	
State the fuel is purchased in:	NY
Fuel type:	Gasoline and undyed diesel fuel.
Refund type:	Operator certified by the New York State Department of Transportation (NYSDOT), Operator certified by the United States Department of Transportation (USDOT), District School Contractor, Carrier operating pursuant to a contract, franchise, or consent with New York City or any agency thereof; or Nonpublic school operator.
Form name:	*Application for Reimbursement of NYS Petroleum Business Tax (PBT) on Motor Fuel/Diesel Motor Fuel for an Omnibus Carrier/Nonpublic School Operator.*
Form #:	**FT-400/401.**
Obtain required forms from:	http://www.tax.ny.gov/forms/pbt_refund_apps_current.htm
Tax deducted from refund:	No.
Tax paid on separate return:	No.
Difficulty:	Difficult.
File by:	3 years from the date of purchase.
Attach documents to claim:	Original sales invoices, delivery tickets, or monthly statements showing the name and address of dealer, name and address of claimant, date of purchase, number of gallons purchased, and the fact that the tax was included in the purchase price are required.
Send to address:	NYS Tax Department Fuel Tax Refund Unit P.O. Box 5501 Albany, NY 12205
Don't file if:	N/A.
State statute(s) supporting refund:	Article 13-A § 301-c.
Keep records on file:	3 years.

New York Fuel Tax Refund Claim Instructions: Petroleum business tax, fuel tax and sales tax refund for fuel purchased for farming equipment.

INSTRUCTIONS	
State the fuel is purchased in:	NY
Fuel type:	Gasoline and undyed diesel fuel.
Refund type:	Farming equipment.
Form name:	*Refund Application for Farmers Purchasing Motor Fuel.*
Form #:	**FT-420.**
Obtain required forms from:	http://www.tax.ny.gov/forms/pbt_refund_apps_current.htm
Tax deducted from refund:	No.
Tax paid on separate return:	No.
Difficulty:	Difficult.
File by:	Claims for reimbursement of the motor fuel or diesel motor fuel excise tax and the petroleum business tax must be filed within 3 years from the date of purchase. Claims for refund of the New York State and local sales tax should be filed within 3 years from the date the tax was due.
Attach documents to claim:	Original invoices signed by the dealer or purchaser's monthly statement, name and address of purchaser, name and address of the dealer, date of purchase, number of gallons, type of fuel, and the motor fuel excise tax, petroleum business tax and sales tax listed separately.
Send to address:	NYS Tax Department Fuel Tax Refund Unit P.O. Box 5501 Albany, NY 12205
Don't file if:	N/A.
State statute(s) supporting refund:	Articles 12-A, 13-A, 28 and 29.
Keep records on file:	3 years.

New York Fuel Tax Refund Claim Instructions: Sales tax refund for fuel purchased for specific exempt organizations, extractors, horse boarding operators, QEZE (qualified empire zone enterprises), manufacturers, miners, Native American-owned equipment, omnibus carriers and refiners.

INSTRUCTIONS	
State the fuel is purchased in:	NY
Fuel type:	Various fuels.
Refund type:	Exempt organizations (except for New York State (NYS) government entities), qualified Indian nations or tribes, farmers or commercial horse boarding operators, qualified empire zone enterprises (QEZE) who use the fuel in qualifying motor vehicles or who use the fuel directly and predominantly (at least 50%) in empire zones where they have qualified to receive benefits, omnibus carriers or vessel operators providing local transit service within NYS, purchasers of fuel used for residential heating , Indians who are enrolled members of an exempt tribe or nation, and who took delivery of the motor fuel or diesel motor fuel on a qualified reservation for their use, manufacturers, processors, generators, assemblers, refiners, miners, and extractors, Other purchase exempt pursuant to Tax Law Section 1115(a).
Form name:	*Application for Refund of Sales Tax Paid on Petroleum Products.*
Form #:	**FT-500.**
Obtain required forms from:	http://www.tax.ny.gov/forms/pbt_refund_apps_current.htm
Tax deducted from refund:	No.
Tax paid on separate return:	No.
Difficulty:	Difficult.
File by:	You must file the application for refund within 3 years from the date the tax was payable to the Tax Department.
Attach documents to claim:	You must submit copies of all invoices on which the claim is based. Invoices must be in the name of the claimant and show the amount of tax paid by the claimant. Receipts that do not identify the claimant as the purchaser are not acceptable.
Send to address:	NYS Tax Department Fuel Tax Refund Unit P.O. Box 5501 Albany, NY 12205
Don't file if:	N/A.
State statute(s) supporting refund:	Articles 12-A, 13-A, 28 and 29.
Keep records on file:	3 years.

<u>New York Fuel Tax Refund Claim Instructions</u>: State and local sales, motor fuel excise and petroleum business tax refund for fuel purchased with a credit card for government-owned vehicles or equipment.

INSTRUCTIONS	
State the fuel is purchased in:	NY
Fuel type:	Gasoline and undyed diesel motor fuel sold to a government agency and paid for with the issuer's credit card.
Refund type:	Fuel sold to state or Federal government agency with a credit card.
Form name:	*Claim for Refund of Taxes Paid on Government Entity Credit Card Purchases of Fuel.*
Form #:	**FT-505.**
Obtain required forms from:	http://www.tax.ny.gov/forms/pbt_refund_apps_current.htm
Tax deducted from refund:	No.
Tax paid on separate return:	No.
Difficulty:	Difficult.
File by:	3 years from the date the fuel was purchased.
Attach documents to claim:	Copies of motor fuel receipts or invoices.
Send to address:	NYS Tax Department Fuel Tax Refund Unit P.O. Box 5501 Albany, NY 12205
Don't file if:	N/A.
State statute(s) supporting refund:	Articles 12-A, 13-A, 28, and 29.
Keep records on file:	3 years.

NORTH CAROLINA

<u>North Carolina Fuel Tax Refund Claim Instructions</u>: Fuel tax refund for fuel purchased for non-profit owned equipment.

INSTRUCTIONS	
State the fuel is purchased in:	NC
Fuel type:	Gasoline, undyed kerosene and undyed diesel fuel.
Refund type:	Volunteer fire departments, volunteer rescue squads and sheltered workshops. Other: Private, nonprofit organizations transporting passengers under contract with or at the express designation of a unit of local government.
Form name:	*Motor Fuels Claim for Refund Nonprofit Organizations.*
Form #:	**GAS-1200.**
Obtain required forms from:	http://www.dor.state.nc.us/downloads/motor.html
Tax deducted from refund:	No.
Tax paid on separate return:	No.
Difficulty:	Moderate.
File by:	3 years from the date the fuel was purchased.
Attach documents to claim:	Copies of fuel invoices are required to be submitted along with the first refund application. Each invoice must show the date of purchase, name and address of the seller, name and address of the purchaser, type of fuel, number of gallons purchased, price per gallon, and the total amount paid. Invoices that show alterations and erasures are not allowed. The Department will not require fuel invoices to be submitted for each refund application thereafter but reserves the right to request them on future refund claims.
Send to address:	North Carolina Department of Revenue Excise Tax Division Post Office Box 25000 Raleigh, North Carolina 27640
Don't file if:	Fuel is purchased and sold to employees, members, returned to the vendor or used for other than official use.
State statute(s) supporting refund:	§ 105-449.106(a).
Keep records on file:	3 years.

North Carolina Fuel Tax Refund Claim Instructions: Fuel tax refund for fuel purchased for selected PTO vehicles.

INSTRUCTIONS	
State the fuel is purchased in:	NC
Fuel type:	Gasoline, undyed kerosene and undyed diesel fuel.
Refund type:	PTO (power take-off) vehicles. Note: Limited to concrete mixing vehicles, solid waste compacting vehicles, tank wagon motor fuel delivery vehicles, mulch-blowing vehicles, bulk feed vehicles, bulk fertilizer vehicles, bulk lime vehicles, seepage removal vehicles, and sweepers.
Form name:	*Motor Fuel Claim for Refund Qualified Power Takeoff Vehicles.*
Form #:	**GAS-1200C.**
Obtain required forms from:	http://www.dor.state.nc.us/downloads/motor.html
Tax deducted from refund:	Yes.
Tax paid on separate return:	No.
Difficulty:	Moderate.
File by:	Claims for refund are due by April 16th for fuel purchases made for the prior year.
Attach documents to claim:	Copies of fuel invoices are required to be submitted along with the first refund application. Each invoice must show the date of purchase, name and address of the seller, name and address of the purchaser, type of fuel, number of gallons purchased, price per gallon, and the total amount paid. Invoices that show alterations and erasures are not allowed. The Department will not require fuel invoices to be submitted for each refund application thereafter but reserves the right to request them on future refund claims.
Send to address:	North Carolina Department of Revenue Excise Tax Division Post Office Box 25000 Raleigh, North Carolina 27640
Don't file if:	N/A.
State statute(s) supporting refund:	§ 105-449.107(b).
Keep records on file:	3 years.

<u>North Carolina Fuel Tax Refund Claim Instructions</u>: Fuel tax refund for fuel purchased for boats, farming equipment, logging equipment and reefer trailers.

INSTRUCTIONS	
State the fuel is purchased in:	NC
Fuel type:	Gasoline, undyed kerosene and undyed diesel fuel.
Refund type:	Commercial boats, farming equipment, logging, and refrigeration (reefer) trailers.
Form name:	*Motor Fuel Claim for Refund Tax-Paid Motor Fuel Used Off-road.*
Form #:	**GAS-1201.**
Obtain required forms from:	http://www.dor.state.nc.us/downloads/motor.html
Tax deducted from refund:	Yes.
Tax paid on separate return:	No.
Difficulty:	Moderate.
File by:	Claims for refund are due by April 16th for fuel purchases made for the prior year. Claims for refund may be filed up to three years from the due date.
Attach documents to claim:	Copies of fuel invoices are required to be submitted along with the first refund application. Each invoice must show the date of purchase, name and address of the seller, name and address of the purchaser, type of fuel, number of gallons purchased, price per gallon, and the total amount paid. Invoices that show alterations and erasures are not allowed. The Department will not require fuel invoices to be submitted for each refund application thereafter but reserves the right to request them on future refund claims.
Send to address:	North Carolina Department of Revenue Excise Tax Division Post Office Box 25000 Raleigh, North Carolina 27640
Don't file if:	N/A.
State statute(s) supporting refund:	§ 105-449.107(a).
Keep records on file:	3 years.

<u>North Carolina Fuel Tax Refund Claim Instructions</u>: Fuel tax refund for fuel purchased for selected PTO vehicles.

INSTRUCTIONS	
State the fuel is purchased in:	NC
Fuel type:	Gasoline, undyed kerosene and undyed diesel fuel.
Refund type:	PTO vehicles. Note: Includes cranes, mills, well-boring apparatus, ditch-digging apparatus, air compressors, electric welders, feed mixers, grinders or other similar apparatus.
Form name:	*Motor Fuels Claim for Refund Special Mobile Equipment.*
Form #:	**GAS-1201ME** Note: Can be filed online at www.dornc.com.
Obtain required forms from:	http://www.dor.state.nc.us/downloads/motor.html
Tax deducted from refund:	Yes.
Tax paid on separate return:	No.
Difficulty:	Moderate.
File by:	Claims for refund are due by April 16th for fuel purchases made for the prior year. Claims for refund may be filed up to three years from the due date.
Attach documents to claim:	Copies of fuel invoices are required to be submitted along with the first refund application. Each invoice must show the date of purchase, name and address of the seller, name and address of the purchaser, type of fuel, number of gallons purchased, price per gallon, and the total amount paid. Invoices that show alterations and erasures are not allowed. The Department will not require fuel invoices to be submitted for each refund application thereafter but reserves the right to request them on future refund claims.
Send to address:	North Carolina Department of Revenue Excise Tax Division Post Office Box 25000 Raleigh, North Carolina 27640
Don't file if:	N/A.
State statute(s) supporting refund:	§ 105-449.106(c).
Keep records on file:	3 years.

<u>North Carolina Fuel Tax Refund Claim Instructions</u>: Fuel tax refund for fuel purchased for government and school-owned vehicles and equipment.

INSTRUCTIONS	
State the fuel is purchased in:	NC
Fuel type:	Gasoline, undyed kerosene and undyed diesel fuel.
Refund type:	Schools, state and Federal government agencies.
Form name:	*Motor Fuel Claim for Refund Exempt Entities.*
Form #:	**GAS-1206.**
Obtain required forms from:	http://www.dor.state.nc.us/downloads/motor.html
Tax deducted from refund:	No.
Tax paid on separate return:	No.
Difficulty:	Moderate.
File by:	Claims for refund are due by the last day of the month followed by the close of the quarter. Claims for refund may be filed up to three years from the due date.
Attach documents to claim:	Copies of fuel invoices are required to be submitted along with the first refund application. Each invoice must show the date of purchase, name and address of the seller, name and address of the purchaser, type of fuel, number of gallons purchased, price per gallon, and the total amount paid. Invoices that show alterations and erasures are not allowed. The Department will not require fuel invoices to be submitted for each refund application thereafter but reserves the right to request them on future refund claims.
Send to address:	North Carolina Department of Revenue Excise Tax Division Post Office Box 25000 Raleigh, North Carolina 27640
Don't file if:	N/A.
State statute(s) supporting refund:	§ 105-449.105.
Keep records on file:	3 years.

North Carolina Fuel Tax Refund Claim Instructions: Fuel tax refund for undyed kerosene sold by distributors for drying (crops), heating and manufacturing purposes.

INSTRUCTIONS	
State the fuel is purchased in:	NC
Fuel type:	Undyed kerosene fuel sold by distributors.
Refund type:	Drying crops, heating purposes and manufacturing.
Form name:	*Kerosene Claim for Refund.*
Form #:	**GAS-1210.**
Obtain required forms from:	http://www.dor.state.nc.us/downloads/motor.html
Tax deducted from refund:	No.
Tax paid on separate return:	No.
Difficulty:	Moderate.
File by:	Claims for refund are due by the 22nd day of the month followed by the end of the month. Claims for refund may be filed up to three years from the due date.
Attach documents to claim:	N/A.
Send to address:	North Carolina Department of Revenue Excise Tax Division Post Office Box 25000 Raleigh, North Carolina 27640
Don't file if:	N/A.
State statute(s) supporting refund:	§ 105-449.105A.
Keep records on file:	3 years.

North Carolina Fuel Tax Refund Claim Instructions: Fuel tax refund for imports.

INSTRUCTIONS	
State the fuel is purchased in:	NC
Fuel type:	Ethanol, gasoline, gasohol, jet fuel, kerosene, methanol and undyed diesel fuel.
Refund type:	Imports.
Form name:	*Licensed Distributor/Importer Hold Harmless.*
Form #:	**GAS-1241.**
Obtain required forms from:	http://www.dor.state.nc.us/downloads/motor.html
Tax deducted from refund:	No.
Tax paid on separate return:	No.
Difficulty:	Moderate.
File by:	Claims for refund are due by the 22nd day after the end of each month.
Attach documents to claim:	N/A.
Send to address:	North Carolina Department of Revenue Excise Tax Division Post Office Box 25000 Raleigh, North Carolina 27640
Don't file if:	N/A.
State statute(s) supporting refund:	§ 105-449.105B.
Keep records on file:	3 years.

NORTH DAKOTA

North Dakota Fuel Tax Refund Claim Instructions: Fuel tax refund for fuel purchased for farming equipment.

INSTRUCTIONS	
State the fuel is purchased in:	ND
Fuel type:	Gasoline and gasohol.
Refund type:	Farming equipment. Notes: This includes raising crops, ranching, beekeeping, tree nurseries, agricultural units of colleges and universities, custom combining, manure spreading, and stack moving operations. Fuel used for an agricultural purpose also includes fuel used in a vehicle, engine, or machine, movable or immovable, operated in whole or in part by internal combustion.
Form name:	*Agriculture - North Dakota Office of State Tax Commissioner Motor Vehicle Fuel Tax Claim For Refund.*
Form #:	**R11**.
Obtain required forms from:	http://www.nd.gov/tax/fuel/forms/
Tax deducted from refund:	Yes.
Tax paid on separate return:	No.
Difficulty:	Moderate.
File by:	Claims for refund are due by June 30th for fuel purchases made for the prior year.
Attach documents to claim:	Original invoices or sales tickets, or certified listings, detailing fuel purchases.
Send to address:	Office of North Dakota State Tax Commissioner 600 E. Boulevard Ave., Dept. 127 Bismarck, ND 58505
Don't file if:	Claim is less than $5.00.
State statute(s) supporting refund:	§ 57-43.1-03.1.
Keep records on file:	3 years.

<u>North Dakota Fuel Tax Refund Claim Instructions</u>: Fuel tax refund for fuel purchased for construction equipment.

INSTRUCTIONS	
State the fuel is purchased in:	ND
Fuel type:	Gasoline and gasohol.
Refund type:	Construction equipment. Notes: Must be used for the construction, reconstruction, off- road use or street maintenance projects.
Form name:	*Construction- North Dakota Office of State Tax Commissioner Motor Vehicle Fuel Tax Claim For Refund.*
Form #:	**R11**.
Obtain required forms from:	http://www.nd.gov/tax/fuel/forms/
Tax deducted from refund:	No.
Tax paid on separate return:	No.
Difficulty:	Moderate.
File by:	Claims for refund are due by June 30th for fuel purchases made for the prior year.
Attach documents to claim:	Original invoices or sales tickets, or certified listings, detailing fuel purchases.
Send to address:	Office of North Dakota State Tax Commissioner 600 E. Boulevard Ave., Dept. 127 Bismarck, ND 58505
Don't file if:	Claim is less than $5.00.
State statute(s) supporting refund:	§ 57-43.1-08.
Keep records on file:	3 years.

<u>North Dakota Fuel Tax Refund Claim Instructions</u>: Fuel tax refund for fuel purchased for construction equipment, golf course equipment, industrial equipment, manufacturing, PTO vehicles, reefer trailers, stationary equipment, well drilling equipment and other specialized equipment.

INSTRUCTIONS	
State the fuel is purchased in:	ND
Fuel type:	Gasoline and gasohol.
Refund type:	Cemeteries, construction equipment, electrical equipment services, golf course equipment, industrial equipment, industrial equipment, loading dock operating equipment, maintenance equipment, manufacturing equipment, painting equipment, PTO (power take-off equipment), refrigeration (reefer) trailers, sand and gravel processing equipment, stationary equipment, warehousing equipment, well drilling equipment, well testing or servicing. Notes: Does not include heating fuel.
Form name:	*Industrial - North Dakota Office of State Tax Commissioner Motor Vehicle Fuel Tax Claim For Refund.*
Form #:	**Form 11**.
Obtain required forms from:	http://www.nd.gov/tax/fuel/forms/
Tax deducted from refund:	Yes.
Tax paid on separate return:	No.
Difficulty:	Moderate.
File by:	June 30th for fuel purchases made for the prior year.
Attach documents to claim:	Original invoices or sales tickets, or certified listings, detailing fuel purchases.
Send to address:	Office of North Dakota State Tax Commissioner 600 E. Boulevard Ave., Dept. 127 Bismarck, ND 58505
Don't file if:	Claim is less than $5.00 or tax deduction reduces refund overmuch.
State statute(s) supporting refund:	§ 57-43.1-03.1.
Keep records on file:	3 years.

North Dakota Fuel Tax Refund Claim Instructions: Fuel tax refund for fuel purchased for aviation purposes.

INSTRUCTIONS	
State the fuel is purchased in:	ND
Fuel type:	Gasoline and jet fuel.
Refund type:	Aviation.
Form name:	*Aviation - North Dakota Office of State Tax Commissioner Motor Vehicle Fuel Tax Claim For Refund.*
Form #:	**R31**.
Obtain required forms from:	http://www.nd.gov/tax/fuel/forms/
Tax deducted from refund:	Yes, Aviation fuel on which a refund of the $.08 per gallon tax is requested and granted is subject to a 4% excise tax in lieu of the per gallon tax. The 4% excise tax is assessed on the cost of the fuel including freight and related charges. If the Federal aviation fuel tax and the state $.08 per gallon tax were included in the cost of the fuel, those taxes should be deducted before computing the 4% excise tax. The 4% excise tax is deducted from the refundable per gallon tax.
Tax paid on separate return:	No.
Difficulty:	Moderate.
File by:	Claims for refund are due by June 30th for fuel purchases made for the prior year.
Attach documents to claim:	Original invoices or sales tickets, or certified listings, detailing fuel purchases.
Send to address:	Office of North Dakota State Tax Commissioner 600 E. Boulevard Ave., Dept. 127 Bismarck, ND 58505
Don't file if:	Claim is less than $5.00 or tax deduction reduces refund overmuch.
State statute(s) supporting refund:	§ 57-43.1-03, 57-43.1-03.1.
Keep records on file:	3 years.

<u>North Dakota Fuel Tax Refund Claim Instructions</u>: Fuel tax refund for fuel purchased for government-owned vehicles

INSTRUCTIONS	
State the fuel is purchased in:	ND
Fuel type:	Gasoline and gasohol.
Refund type:	Federal government.
Form name:	*Government-Motor Vehicle Fuel Tax Claim For Refund by Federal Agency.*
Form #:	**R11**.
Obtain required forms from:	http://www.nd.gov/tax/fuel/forms/
Tax deducted from refund:	No.
Tax paid on separate return:	No.
Difficulty:	Moderate.
File by:	Claims for refund are due by June 30th for fuel purchases made for the prior year.
Attach documents to claim:	Original invoices or sales tickets, or certified listings, detailing fuel purchases.
Send to address:	Office of North Dakota State Tax Commissioner 600 E. Boulevard Ave., Dept. 127 Bismarck, ND 58505
Don't file if:	Claim is less than $5.00.
State statute(s) supporting refund:	§ 57-43.1-06.1.
Keep records on file:	3 years.

North Dakota Fuel Tax Refund Claim Instructions: Fuel tax refund for undyed diesel purchased for ambulances.

INSTRUCTIONS	
State the fuel is purchased in:	ND
Fuel type:	Undyed diesel fuel.
Refund type:	Ambulances. Notes: This does not include fuel used in multi-purpose vehicles, non-ambulance hospital or nursing home vehicles.
Form name:	*North Dakota Office of State Tax Commissioner Special Fuel Tax Claim For Refund.*
Form #:	**EMS Tax Type 62.**
Obtain required forms from:	http://www.nd.gov/tax/fuel/forms/
Tax deducted from refund:	No.
Tax paid on separate return:	No.
Difficulty:	Moderate.
File by:	Claims for refund are due by June 30th for fuel purchases made for the prior year.
Attach documents to claim:	Original invoices or sales tickets, or certified listings, detailing fuel purchases.
Send to address:	Office of North Dakota State Tax Commissioner 600 E. Boulevard Ave., Dept. 127 Bismarck, ND 58505
Don't file if:	Claim is less than $5.00. Refunds are also not allowed on fuel used in multi-purpose vehicles owned by municipalities or non-ambulance hospital and nursing home vehicles.
State statute(s) supporting refund:	§ 57-43.1-03.3.
Keep records on file:	3 years.

<u>North Dakota Fuel Tax Refund Claim Instructions</u>: Fuel tax refund for motor vehicle fuel purchased for ambulances.

INSTRUCTIONS	
State the fuel is purchased in:	ND
Fuel type:	Gasoline and gasohol.
Refund type:	Fuel used by an operator of an emergency medical services operation for fuel used in ambulances. This does not include fuel used in multi-purpose vehicles, non-ambulance hospital or nursing home vehicles.
Form name:	*North Dakota Office of State Tax Commissioner Motor Vehicle Tax Claim For Refund.*
Form #:	**EMS Tax Type 61.**
Obtain required forms from:	http://www.nd.gov/tax/fuel/forms/
Tax deducted from refund:	No.
Tax paid on separate return:	No.
Difficulty:	Moderate.
File by:	Claims for refund are due by June 30th for fuel purchases made for the prior year.
Attach documents to claim:	Original invoices or sales tickets, or certified listings, detailing fuel purchases.
Send to address:	Office of North Dakota State Tax Commissioner 600 E. Boulevard Ave., Dept. 127 Bismarck, ND 58505
Don't file if:	Claim is less than $5.00.
State statute(s) supporting refund:	§ 57-43.1-03.3.
Keep records on file:	3 years.

<u>North Dakota Fuel Tax Refund Claim Instructions</u>: Fuel tax refund for jet fuel or gasoline purchased for planes used for a medical purpose.

INSTRUCTIONS	
State the fuel is purchased in:	ND
Fuel type:	Aviation gasoline and jet fuel.
Refund type:	An operator of an emergency medical services operation may claim a refund of state special fuel taxes on fuel used in a vehicle specifically for an emergency medical service operation.
Form name:	*EMS Aviation Fuel Tax Claim For Refund.*
Form #:	**EMS Tax Type 53.**
Obtain required forms from:	http://www.nd.gov/tax/fuel/forms/
Tax deducted from refund:	No.
Tax paid on separate return:	No.
Difficulty:	Moderate.
File by:	Claims for refund are due by June 30th for fuel purchases made for the prior year.
Attach documents to claim:	Original invoices or sales tickets, or certified listings, detailing fuel purchases.
Send to address:	Office of North Dakota State Tax Commissioner 600 E. Boulevard Ave., Dept. 127 Bismarck, ND 58505
Don't file if:	Claim is less than $5.00. Refunds are also not allowed on fuel used in multi-purpose vehicles owned by municipalities or non-ambulance hospital and nursing home vehicles.
State statute(s) supporting refund:	§ 57-43.1-03.3.
Keep records on file:	3 years.

North Dakota Fuel Tax Refund Claim Instructions: Fuel tax refund for motor fuel purchased for vehicles owned by Native Americans.

INSTRUCTIONS	
State the fuel is purchased in:	ND
Fuel type:	Gasoline and gasohol.
Refund type:	Native American-owned vehicles.
Form name:	*Claim for Motor Vehicle Fuel Tax Refund by Native American Tribal Agency.*
Form #:	No Form No.
Obtain required forms from:	http://www.nd.gov/tax/fuel/forms/
Tax deducted from refund:	No.
Tax paid on separate return:	No.
Difficulty:	Moderate.
File by:	Claims for refund are due by June 30th for fuel purchases made for the prior year.
Attach documents to claim:	Original invoices or sales tickets, or certified listings, detailing fuel purchases.
Send to address:	Office of North Dakota State Tax Commissioner 600 E. Boulevard Ave., Dept. 127 Bismarck, ND 58505
Don't file if:	Claim is less than $5.00.
State statute(s) supporting refund:	§ 57-43.1-03.2.
Keep records on file:	3 years.

North Dakota Fuel Tax Refund Claim Instructions: Fuel tax refund for undyed fuel purchased for vehicles owned by Native Americans.

INSTRUCTIONS	
State the fuel is purchased in:	ND
Fuel type:	Undyed diesel fuel.
Refund type:	Native American-owned vehicles.
Form name:	*Claim for Special Fuel Tax Refund by Native American Tribal Agency.*
Form #:	No Form No.
Obtain required forms from:	http://www.nd.gov/tax/fuel/forms/
Tax deducted from refund:	No.
Tax paid on separate return:	No.
Difficulty:	Moderate.
File by:	Claims for refund are due by June 30th for fuel purchases made for the prior year.
Attach documents to claim:	Original invoices or sales tickets, or certified listings, detailing fuel purchases.
Send to address:	Office of North Dakota State Tax Commissioner 600 E. Boulevard Ave., Dept. 127 Bismarck, ND 58505
Don't file if:	Claim is less than $5.00.
State statute(s) supporting refund:	§ 57-43.1-03.2.
Keep records on file:	3 years.

<u>North Dakota Fuel Tax Refund Claim Instructions</u>: Fuel tax refund for undyed fuel purchased for reefer trailers.

INSTRUCTIONS	
State the fuel is purchased in:	ND
Fuel type:	Undyed diesel fuel.
Refund type:	Refrigeration (reefer) trailers.
Form name:	*Special Fuel Tax Claim For Refund.*
Form #:	**R11 Refrigeration**.
Obtain required forms from:	http://www.nd.gov/tax/fuel/forms/
Tax deducted from refund:	Yes.
Tax paid on separate return:	No.
Difficulty:	Moderate.
File by:	Claims for refund are due by June 30th for fuel purchases made for the prior year.
Attach documents to claim:	Original invoices or sales tickets, or certified listings, detailing fuel purchases.
Send to address:	Office of North Dakota State Tax Commissioner 600 E. Boulevard Ave., Dept. 127 Bismarck, ND 58505
Don't file if:	Claim is less than $5.00 or tax deduction reduces refund overmuch.
State statute(s) supporting refund:	§ 57-43.1-03.3.
Keep records on file:	3 years.

<u>North Dakota Fuel Tax Refund Claim Instructions</u>: Fuel tax refund for aviation fuel or gasoline used for an exempt purpose by an unlicensed retailer.

INSTRUCTIONS	
State the fuel is purchased in:	ND
Fuel type:	Aviation gasoline and jet fuel.
Refund type:	Other: Aviation fuel tax where the claimant is a retailer and does not have a valid aviation fuel tax license. If fuel taxes are paid by a retailer to a supplier or distributor, and non-taxed sales are made to a Federal agency, the taxes are fully refundable to the retailer.
Form name:	*Aviation Fuel Tax Claim for Refund by Non-licensed Retailer.*
Form #:	No Form No.
Obtain required forms from:	http://www.nd.gov/tax/fuel/forms/
Tax deducted from refund:	No.
Tax paid on separate return:	No.
Difficulty:	Moderate.
File by:	Claims for refund are due by June 30th for fuel purchases made for the prior year.
Attach documents to claim:	Copies of motor fuel invoices or a certified listing.
Send to address:	Office of North Dakota State Tax Commissioner 600 E. Boulevard Ave., Dept. 127 Bismarck, ND 58505
Don't file if:	Claim is less than $400.00.
State statute(s) supporting refund:	§ 57-43.1-03, 57-43.1-03.1.
Keep records on file:	3 years.

<u>North Dakota Fuel Tax Refund Claim Instructions</u>: Fuel tax refund for retailers of gasoline sold for an exempt purpose.

INSTRUCTIONS	
State the fuel is purchased in:	ND
Fuel type:	Gasoline and gasohol.
Refund type:	Fuel tax paid by claimant where claimant is a retailer and does not have a valid motor vehicle fuel tax license. If fuel taxes are paid by a retailer to a supplier or distributor, and non-taxed sales are made to a Federal agency, the taxes are fully refundable to the retailer.
Form name:	*Motor Vehicle Fuel Tax Claim for Refund by Non-licensed Retailer.*
Form #:	No Form No.
Obtain required forms from:	http://www.nd.gov/tax/fuel/forms/
Tax deducted from refund:	No.
Tax paid on separate return:	No.
Difficulty:	Moderate.
File by:	Claims for refund are due by June 30th for fuel purchases made for the prior year.
Attach documents to claim:	The claimant must provide detailed proof of purchase and proof of tax payments with each claim. The proof may be in the form of individual invoices or a certified listing.
Send to address:	Office of North Dakota State Tax Commissioner 600 E. Boulevard Ave., Dept. 127 Bismarck, ND 58505
Don't file if:	Claim is less than $400.00.
State statute(s) supporting refund:	§ 57-43.1-03, 57-43.1-03.1.
Keep records on file:	3 years.

North Dakota Fuel Tax Refund Claim Instructions: Fuel tax refund for retailers of undyed diesel fuel sold for an exempt purpose.

INSTRUCTIONS	
State the fuel is purchased in:	ND
Fuel type:	Undyed diesel fuel.
Refund type:	Fuel tax paid by claimant where claimant is a retailer and does not have a valid motor vehicle fuel tax license. If fuel taxes are paid by a retailer to a supplier or distributor, and non-taxed sales are made to a Federal agency, the taxes are fully refundable to the retailer.
Form name:	*Special Fuel Tax Claim for Refund by Nonlicensed Retailer.*
Form #:	No Form No.
Obtain required forms from:	http://www.nd.gov/tax/fuel/forms/
Tax deducted from refund:	No.
Tax paid on separate return:	No.
Difficulty:	Moderate.
File by:	Claims for refund are due by June 30th for fuel purchases made for the prior year.
Attach documents to claim:	The claimant must provide detailed proof of purchase and proof of tax payments with each claim. The proof may be in the form of individual invoices or a certified listing.
Send to address:	Office of North Dakota State Tax Commissioner 600 E. Boulevard Ave., Dept. 127 Bismarck, ND 58505
Don't file if:	Claim is less than $400.00.
State statute(s) supporting refund:	§ 57-43.1-03, 57-43.1-03.1.
Keep records on file:	3 years.

OHIO

Ohio Fuel Tax Refund Claim Instructions: Fuel tax refund for fuel purchased for school-owned vehicles or equipment.

INSTRUCTIONS	
State the fuel is purchased in:	OH
Fuel type:	Gasoline, LPG (liquid petroleum gas), propane and undyed diesel fuel. Note: CNG (compressed natural gas) is non-taxable and does not qualify for a refund.
Refund type:	School buses. Note: All public school (including JVS) or ESC operations will qualify for a refund (e.g., transportation of students, operation of service vehicles, lawn mowers). The fuel purchased by the transportation company does not qualify for refund. Fuel purchased by the school district and provided to a transportation company for school or ESC operations qualifies for refund.
Form name:	Various, see below.
Form #:	**MVF-31**, *Application for Fuel Tax Refund.* Upon receipt of the completed application, your school district will be issued a refund permit number, and you will be sent your first MVF-81 (Ohio Motor Fuel Tax Refund Claim for School Districts) refund claim.
Obtain required forms from:	Call Ohio Department of Taxation.
Tax deducted from refund:	No.
Tax paid on separate return:	No.
Difficulty:	Moderate.
File by:	365 days from the date of fuel purchase.
Attach documents to claim:	Copies of motor fuel receipts or invoices, or any other document that contains the name and address of the seller, name of the purchaser, date of purchase, type of fuel, the number of gallons purchased and the purchase price.
Send to address:	Ohio Department of Taxation Motor Fuel Tax Refund Unit P.O. Box 530 Columbus, OH 43216
Don't file if:	Claim is for less than 100 gallons.
State statute(s) supporting refund:	§ 5735.142.
Keep records on file:	4 years.

<u>Ohio Fuel Tax Refund Claim Instructions</u>: Fuel tax refund fuel purchased for mass transit buses.

INSTRUCTIONS	
State the fuel is purchased in:	OH
Fuel type:	Gasoline, LPG (liquid petroleum gas), propane and undyed diesel fuel. Note: CNG (compressed natural gas) is non-taxable and does not qualify for a refund.
Refund type:	Mass transit buses.
Form name:	*Ohio Motor Fuel Tax Refund Claim for Transit Buses*.
Form #:	**MVF-9.**
Obtain required forms from:	Call the Ohio Department of Taxation.
Tax deducted from refund:	No.
Tax paid on separate return:	No.
Difficulty:	Moderate.
File by:	365 days from the date of fuel purchase.
Attach documents to claim:	Copies of motor fuel receipts or invoices, or any other document that contains the name and address of the seller, name of the purchaser, date of purchase, type of fuel, the number of gallons purchased and the purchase price.
Send to address:	Ohio Department of Taxation Motor Fuel Tax Refund Unit P.O. Box 530 Columbus, OH 43216
Don't file if:	Claim is for less than 100 gallons.
State statute(s) supporting refund:	§ 5735.142.
Keep records on file:	4 years.

<u>Ohio Fuel Tax Refund Claim Instructions</u>: Fuel tax refund for fuel purchased for boats.

INSTRUCTIONS	
State the fuel is purchased in:	OH
Fuel type:	Gasoline, LPG (liquid petroleum gas), propane and undyed diesel fuel. Note: CNG (compressed natural gas) is non-taxable and does not qualify for a refund.
Refund type:	Commercial boats.
Form name:	Various, see below.
Form #:	*Request Form From Ohio Department of Taxation.* **MVF-31**, *Application for Fuel Tax Refund*. Upon receipt of the completed application, filer will be issued a refund permit number, and sent your first Ohio refund claim.
Obtain required forms from:	Call the Ohio Department of Taxation.
Tax deducted from refund:	Yes.
Tax paid on separate return:	No.
Difficulty:	Difficult.
File by:	365 days from the date of fuel purchase.
Attach documents to claim:	Copies of motor fuel receipts or invoices, or any other document that contains the name and address of the seller, name of the purchaser, date of purchase, type of fuel, the number of gallons purchased and the purchase price.
Send to address:	Ohio Department of Taxation Motor Fuel Tax Refund Unit P.O. Box 530 Columbus, OH 43216
Don't file if:	Claim is for less than 100 gallons.
State statute(s) supporting refund:	§ 5735.14.
Keep records on file:	4 years.

Ohio Fuel Tax Refund Claim Instructions: Fuel tax refund for fuel purchased for PTO vehicles.

INSTRUCTIONS	
State the fuel is purchased in:	OH
Fuel type:	Gasoline, LPG (liquid petroleum gas), propane and undyed diesel fuel. Note: CNG (compressed natural gas) is non-taxable and does not qualify for a refund.
Refund type:	PTO (power take-off) vehicles.
Form name:	*Request Form From Ohio Department of Taxation.*
Form #:	**MVF-31**, *Application for Fuel Tax Refund.* Note: Upon receipt of the completed application, filer will be issued a refund permit number, and sent your first Ohio refund claim.
Obtain required forms from:	Call the Ohio Department of Taxation.
Tax deducted from refund:	Yes.
Tax paid on separate return:	No.
Difficulty:	Difficult.
File by:	The claim must be filed within 365 days from the date of fuel purchase.
Attach documents to claim:	Copies of motor fuel receipts or invoices, or any other document that contains the name and address of the seller, name of the purchaser, date of purchase, type of fuel, the number of gallons purchased and the purchase price.
Send to address:	Ohio Department of Taxation Motor Fuel Tax Refund Unit P.O. Box 530 Columbus, OH 43216
Don't file if:	Claim is for less than 100 gallons.
State statute(s) supporting refund:	§ 5735.14.
Keep records on file:	4 years.

Ohio Fuel Tax Refund Claim Instructions: Fuel tax refund for fuel purchased for farming equipment.

INSTRUCTIONS	
State the fuel is purchased in:	OH
Fuel type:	Gasoline, LPG (liquid petroleum gas), propane and undyed diesel fuel. Note: CNG (compressed natural gas) is non-taxable and does not qualify for a refund.
Refund type:	Farming equipment.
Form name:	Various, see below.
Form #:	The **MVF-4 AG,** *Agriculture claim* is only available by filing an **MVF-31,** *Motor Fuel Refund Permit Application*, and referencing the proper fuel tax exemption in the application.
Obtain required forms from:	Call the Ohio Department of Taxation.
Tax deducted from refund:	Yes.
Tax paid on separate return:	No.
Difficulty:	Difficult.
File by:	The claim must be filed within 365 days from the date of fuel purchase.
Attach documents to claim:	Copies of motor fuel receipts or invoices, or any other document that contains the name and address of the seller, name of the purchaser, date of purchase, type of fuel, the number of gallons purchased and the purchase price.
Send to address:	Ohio Department of Taxation Motor Fuel Tax Refund Unit P.O. Box 530 Columbus, OH 43216
Don't file if:	Claim is for less than 100 gallons.
State statute(s) supporting refund:	§ 5735.14.
Keep records on file:	4 years.

<u>Ohio Fuel Tax Refund Claim Instructions</u>: Fuel tax refund for fuel purchased for industrial equipment.

INSTRUCTIONS	
State the fuel is purchased in:	OH
Fuel type:	Gasoline, LPG (liquid petroleum gas), propane and undyed diesel fuel. Note: CNG (compressed natural gas) is non-taxable and does not qualify for a refund.
Refund type:	Industrial equipment.
Form name:	Various, see below.
Form #:	The **MVF-4 IND** claim is only available by filing an **MVF-31** *Motor Fuel Refund Permit Application*, and referencing the proper fuel tax exemption in the application.
Obtain required forms from:	Call the Ohio Department of Taxation.
Tax deducted from refund:	Yes.
Tax paid on separate return:	No.
Difficulty:	Difficult.
File by:	The claim must be filed within 365 days from the date of fuel purchase.
Attach documents to claim:	Copies of motor fuel receipts or invoices, or any other document that contains the name and address of the seller, name of the purchaser, date of purchase, type of fuel, the number of gallons purchased, and the purchase price, must be submitted with this claim.
Send to address:	Ohio Department of Taxation Motor Fuel Tax Refund Unit P.O. Box 530 Columbus, OH 43216
Don't file if:	Claim is for less than 100 gallons.
State statute(s) supporting refund:	§ 5735.14.
Keep records on file:	4 years.

<u>Ohio Fuel Tax Refund Claim Instructions</u>: Fuel tax refund for purchasers of fuel that has been lost due to environmental and man-made factors.

INSTRUCTIONS	
State the fuel is purchased in:	OH
Fuel type:	Gasoline, LPG (liquid petroleum gas), propane and undyed diesel fuel. Note: CNG (compressed natural gas) is non-taxable and does not qualify for a refund.
Refund type:	Fuel shrinkage and evaporation. Note: Any retail dealer of motor fuel shall receive a refund for Ohio motor fuel taxes paid on fuel lost by a retail dealer through shrinkage and evaporation. A refund shall be made to any person for the motor fuel tax paid on any motor fuel that is lost or destroyed through leakage, fire, explosion, lightning, flood, tornado, windstorm, or any other cause, except theft, evaporation, shrinkage, and unaccounted-for losses.
Form name:	*Request Form From Ohio Department of Taxation.*
Form #:	**MVF-31** (Application for Fuel Tax Refund) Upon receipt of the completed application, filer will be issued a refund permit number, and sent your first Ohio refund claim.
Obtain required forms from:	Call the Ohio Department of Taxation.
Tax deducted from refund:	Yes.
Tax paid on separate return:	No.
Difficulty:	Difficult.
File by:	120 after the 30th day of June and the 31st day of December of each year, an application for a refund stating the quantity of motor fuel that was purchased for resale by the applicant during the preceding semiannual period ending the 30th day of June or the 31st day of December and upon which the motor fuel tax has been paid.
Attach documents to claim:	Copies of motor fuel receipts or invoices, or any other document that contains the name and address of the seller, name of the purchaser, date of purchase, type of fuel, the number of gallons purchased, and the purchase price, must be submitted with this claim.
Send to address:	Ohio Department of Taxation Motor Fuel Tax Refund Unit P.O. Box 530 Columbus, OH 43216
Don't file if:	Claim is for less than 100 gallons.
State statute(s) supporting refund:	§ 5735.141.
Keep records on file:	4 years.

OKLAHOMA

<u>Oklahoma Fuel Tax Refund Claim Instructions</u>: Fuel tax refund by purchasers of fuel used in construction equipment, contamination / loss, exports, farming equipment, government-owned vehicles, heating, idling, off-road use, oilfield equipment, planes, reefer trailers, school buses and other stationary equipment.

INSTRUCTIONS	
State the fuel is purchased in:	OK
Fuel type:	Aviation fuel, gasoline and undyed diesel fuel.
Refund type:	Construction equipment, contamination / loss, exports, farming equipment, heating, idling, Native American, off-road use, oilfield equipment, planes, PTO (power take-off) vehicles, refrigeration (reefer) trailers, school buses, state and Federal government agencies, stationary equipment and trains.
Form name:	*Oklahoma Tax Commission Application for Refund of Motor Fuel Tax Gasoline and Undyed Diesel Only.*
Form #:	**Form 130.**
Obtain required forms from:	http://www.tax.ok.gov/mfforms.html
Tax deducted from refund:	Yes.
Tax paid on separate return:	Yes, the sales tax is due on the 20th day following the month in which the refund is issued and could exceed the amount of the diesel fuel tax refund.
Difficulty:	Difficult.
File by:	3 years following the last day of the calendar month in which the fuel tax was paid.
Attach documents to claim:	Documentation of loss must accompany application. For Purchasers who erroneously paid the motor fuel tax. Documentation of exempt status must accompany application.
Send to address:	Oklahoma Tax Commission Account Maintenance Division Credits and Refunds Section 2501 Lincoln Boulevard Oklahoma City, OK 73194
Don't file if:	Sales7 tax is greater than refund or claim is less than $25.00 for any given period.
State statute(s) supporting refund:	§68-500.10.
Keep records on file:	3 years.

<u>Oklahoma Fuel Tax Refund Claim Instru7ctions</u>: Fuel tax refund for natural gas purchased for farming, Native American – owned vehicles, school buses and government-owned vehicles.

INSTRUCTIONS	
State the fuel is purchased in:	OK
Fuel type:	CNG (compressed natural gas).
Refund type:	Farming equipment, stationary equipment, Native American, schools and state and Federal government agencies.
Form name:	*Oklahoma Tax Commission Application for Refund of CNG (Compressed Natural Gas)*
Form #:	**70001.**
Obtain required forms from:	http://www.tax.ok.gov/mfforms.html
Tax deducted from refund:	Yes.
Tax paid on separate return:	Yes.
Difficulty:	Easy.
File by:	3 years following the last day of the calendar month in which the fuel tax was paid.
Attach documents to claim:	N/A.
Send to address:	Oklahoma Tax Commission Account Maintenance Division/Credits and Refunds Section 2501 Lincoln Boulevard Oklahoma City, OK 73194
Don't file if:	Sales tax is greater than refund or claim is less than $25.00 for any given period.
State statute(s) supporting refund:	§68-500.10.
Keep records on file:	3 years.

Oklahoma Fuel Tax Refund Claim Instructions: Fuel tax return credit by ethanol retailers.

INSTRUCTIONS	
State the fuel is purchased in:	OK
Fuel type:	Ethanol fuel.
Refund type:	Ethanol credit is available to retail dealers who sell fuel grade ethanol to the consumer who uses the motor fuel on the public highways of this state and that the cost savings is economically provided to such consumer of the ethanol fuel.
Form name:	*Application for Refund of Ethanol Credit for Retail Dealers.*
Form #:	**OTC Form 130-35.**
Obtain required forms from:	http://www.tax.ok.gov/mfforms.html
Tax deducted from refund:	No.
Tax paid on separate return:	No.
Difficulty:	Easy.
File by:	3 years following the last day of the calendar month in which the fuel tax was paid.
Attach documents to claim:	None.
Send to address:	Oklahoma Tax Commission Account Maintenance Division/Credits and Refunds Section 2501 Lincoln Boulevard Oklahoma City, OK 73194
Don't file if:	N/A.
State statute(s) supporting refund:	Title 68, O.S. 500.10-1, effective 01/01/2006.
Keep records on file:	3 years.

OREGON

<u>Oregon Fuel Tax Refund Claim Instructions</u>: Fuel tax refund for fuel purchased for ATV's, cleaning, commercial boating use, construction, dyeing, exports, farming, golf course equipment, government-owned vehicles, lawn equipment, logging, off-road use, oilfield equipment, planes, PTO vehicles, reefer trailers, snowmobiles and other stationary equipment.

INSTRUCTIONS	
State the fuel is purchased in:	OR
Fuel type:	Gasoline and undyed diesel fuel.
Refund type:	ATVs (all-terrain vehicles) on privately-owned property, cleaning, commercial marine use, construction, dyeing, exports, farming, golf course equipment, lawn equipment, off-road use, planes, PTO (power take-off equipment), removing forest products over certain public roads, oilfield equipment, snowmobiles, state and Federal government agencies and stationary equipment. Note: For PTO vehicles, refund is only available for gasoline when a pre-approved metering device to measure gallons is installed.
Form name:	*Fuels Tax Refund Claim.*
Form #:	Form **1200**, Obtain form **1203** to claim refund for use in aircraft.
Obtain required forms from:	http://www.oregon.gov/ODOT/CS/FTG/ftr.shtml
Tax deducted from refund:	No.
Tax paid on separate return:	No.
Difficulty:	Moderate.
File by:	15 months from the date the fuel was purchased.
Attach documents to claim:	Original motor fuel receipts or invoices. If you have bulk storage, attach original invoices for deliveries to all tanks. Sort invoices into date order with the oldest on top.
Send to address:	ODOT Fuels Tax Group 550 Capitol St. NE Salem, OR 97301
Don't file if:	N/A.
State statute(s) supporting refund:	§319.240 (Exemption of export fuel). §319.831 (Refund of tax on fuel used in operation of vehicle over certain roads or private property). §319.330 (Refunds to purchasers of fuel for aircraft). §319.280 (Refunds generally). §319.320 (Refund of tax on fuel used in operation of vehicles over certain roads or private property).
Keep records on file:	6 years.

PENNSYLVANIA

<u>Pennsylvania Fuel Tax Refund Claim Instructions</u>: Fuel tax refund for fuel purchased for reefer trailers.

INSTRUCTIONS	
State the fuel is purchased in:	PA
Fuel type:	Kerosene and undyed diesel fuel.
Refund type:	Refrigeration (reefer) trailers.
Form name:	*Motor Fuels Tax Reimbursement Claim Form for Undyed Diesel and Undyed Kerosene Used in Truck Refrigeration Units.*
Form #:	**REV-643.**
Obtain required forms from:	http://www.portal.state.pa.us/portal/server.pt/community/motor_fuels_tax/14700
Tax deducted from refund:	No.
Tax paid on separate return:	Yes.
Difficulty:	Easy.
File by:	Carriers must submit reimbursement claims (postmarked) on or before the 60th day following the end of each calendar quarter.
Attach documents to claim:	Copies of fuel purchase invoices for one of the months above or as otherwise directed by the Department must be submitted with this claim.
Send to address:	Bureau of Motor Fuel Taxes. P.O. Box 280646 Harrisburg, PA 17128
Don't file if:	Sales tax is greater than refund.
State statute(s) supporting refund:	Title 75, Chapter 90, C.S. § 9017.
Keep records on file:	3 years.

Pennsylvania Fuel Tax Refund Claim Instructions: Fuel tax refund for fuel purchased for mass transit.

INSTRUCTIONS	
State the fuel is purchased in:	PA
Fuel type:	Gasoline, kerosene and undyed diesel fuel.
Refund type:	Motorbus. Note: A "motorbus" is defined as having: • three or more axles, or a registered gross weight in excess of 26,000 pounds; and • seating capacity of 20 or more passengers, excluding the driver. Further, for purposes of this claim, school buses are not considered motorbuses.
Form name:	*Bus Company Reimbursement Request - For The Additional Oil Company Franchise Tax on Fuels*
Form #:	**REV-642.**
Obtain required forms from:	http://www.portal.state.pa.us/portal/server.pt/community/motor_fuels_tax/14700
Tax deducted from refund:	No.
Tax paid on separate return:	No.
Difficulty:	Moderate.
File by:	The last day of the month immediately following the close of each quarter (i.e. April 30, July 31, Oct 31 or Jan 31).
Attach documents to claim:	A copy of the IFTA quarterly report for which a refund is being requested for an Out-of-State IFTA Bus company.
Send to address:	Bureau of Motor Fuel Taxes. P.O. Box 280646 Harrisburg, PA 17128
Don't file if:	Claimant is filing for fuel used in a school bus.
State statute(s) supporting refund:	Title 75, Chapter 98, C.S. § 9805.
Keep records on file:	3 years.

<u>Pennsylvania Fuel Tax Refund Claim Instructions</u>: Fuel tax refund for fuel purchased for PTO equipment for agricultural usage.

INSTRUCTIONS	
State the fuel is purchased in:	PA
Fuel type:	Gasoline, gasohol and undyed diesel fuel.
Refund type:	PTO (power take-off) vehicles used for agricultural purposes. Note: Agricultural purposes include loading feed, feed products, lime or limestone products for agricultural use in Pennsylvania for delivery to a farm or unloading at a farm in Pennsylvania.
Form name:	*PA Motor Fuels Tax Reimbursement Claim for Power Take-Off Equipment; Agricultural Use of Feed, Feed Products, Lime and Limestone Products.*
Form #:	**DMF-75.**
Obtain required forms from:	http://www.portal.state.pa.us/portal/server.pt/community/motor_fuels_tax/14700
Tax deducted from refund:	Yes.
Tax paid on separate return:	Yes, sales tax should be calculated on the net purchase price (purchase price less tax received as a refund) of the gallons for which a carrier has received a refund and then remitted to the Commonwealth electronically via e-TIDES or TeleFile, unless the carrier's use of the fuel qualifies for a Sales/Use Tax business exemption.
Difficulty:	Easy.
File by:	Carriers must submit reimbursement claims (postmarked) on or before the 60th day following the end of each calendar quarter.
Attach documents to claim:	Copies of fuel purchase invoices. Usage must be documented by an electronic monitoring device used in conjunction with an electronically controlled engine.
Send to address:	Bureau of Motor Fuel Taxes. P.O. Box 280646 Harrisburg, PA 17128
Don't file if:	Sales tax is greater than refund.
State statute(s) supporting refund:	Title 75, Chapter 90, C.S. § 9017.
Keep records on file:	3 years.

<u>Pennsylvania Fuel Tax Refund Claim Instructions</u>: Fuel tax refund for fuel purchased for government-owned equipment.

INSTRUCTIONS	
State the fuel is purchased in:	PA
Fuel type:	Gasoline, gasohol, undyed kerosene and undyed diesel fuel sold by non-permitted dealers and retailers of motor fuels.
Refund type:	State and Federal government agencies.
Form name:	Various, see below.
Form #:	Required form(s): **DMF-80**, *Reimbursement Request for Motor Fuel Taxes Paid on Sales to Government/Exempt Entities.* **REV-568**, *Assignment of Rights – Liquid Fuels and Fuels Tax Refund.*
Obtain required forms from:	http://www.portal.state.pa.us/portal/server.pt/community/motor_fuels_tax/14700
Tax deducted from refund:	No.
Tax paid on separate return:	No.
Difficulty:	Moderate.
File by:	Carriers must submit reimbursement claims (postmarked) on or before the 60th day following the end of each calendar quarter.
Attach documents to claim:	Copies of fuel purchase invoices.
Send to address:	Bureau of Motor Fuel Taxes. P.O. Box 280646 Harrisburg, PA 17128
Don't file if:	Non-permitted dealers/retailers may petition for reimbursement on a quarterly, semi-annual or annual basis. The department will also consider monthly petitions in cases where tax reimbursements exceed $500.
State statute(s) supporting refund:	PA Vehicle Code Section Title 75, Chapter 90, C.S. § 9004.
Keep records on file:	3 years.

RHODE ISLAND

<u>Rhode Island Fuel Tax Refund Claim Instructions</u>: Fuel tax refund for fuel purchased for boats, farming equipment, government-owned vehicles, logging, manufacturing, planes, trains and stationary equipment.

INSTRUCTIONS	
State the fuel is purchased in:	RI
Fuel type:	Gasoline, undyed diesel, LPG (liquid petroleum gas) and other volatile and inflammable liquids used or suitable for use for operating or propelling motor vehicles.
Refund type:	Boats, commercial fishermen, farming, logging, manufacturing, planes, state and Federal government agencies, stationary equipment and trains.
Form name:	*Claim for refund of motor fuel tax.*
Form #:	**T-59.**
Obtain required forms from:	http://www.tax.ri.gov/taxforms/sales_excise/motor_fuel.php
Tax deducted from refund:	No.
Tax paid on separate return:	No.
Difficulty:	Easy.
File by:	240 days from the date the fuel was purchased.
Attach documents to claim:	Original motor fuel receipts or invoices.
Send to address:	Rhode Island Division of Taxation One Capitol Hill Providence, RI 02908
Don't file if:	Claim is for less than $1.00.
State statute(s) supporting refund:	§ 31-36-13, 31-36-15.
Keep records on file:	4 years.

SOUTH CAROLINA

<u>South Carolina Fuel Tax Refund Claim Instructions</u>: Fuel tax refund for fuel purchased for commercial boats, government-owned vehicles, fuel diversions, RTA owned equipment and school buses.

INSTRUCTIONS	
State the fuel is purchased in:	SC
Fuel type:	Gasoline, kerosene, undyed low sulfur and undyed diesel fuel.
Refund type:	Commercial fishing, contamination / loss, Federal government agencies, fuel diversions, sales to or purchases by a RTA (regional transportation authority) and school buses.
Form name:	*Motor Fuel Refund Application.*
Form #:	**L-2133.** Note: File refund application form on initial claim.
Obtain required forms from:	http://www.sctax.org/Forms+and+Instructions/2011/ motorFuel/default.htm
Tax deducted from refund:	No.
Tax paid on separate return:	No.
Difficulty:	Easy.
File by:	3 years from the date the fuel was purchased.
Attach documents to claim:	Copies of motor fuel receipts or invoices.
Send to address:	South Carolina Department of Revenue Motor Fuel Columbia, SC 29214
Don't file if:	N/A.
State statute(s) supporting refund:	§ 12-28-710.
Keep records on file:	3 years.

South Carolina Fuel Tax Refund Claim Instructions: Fuel tax refund for gasoline purchased for planes.

INSTRUCTIONS	
State the fuel is purchased in:	SC
Fuel type:	Gasoline.
Refund type:	Planes.
Form name:	*Refund for Gasoline Use for Aviation Purposes*.
Form #:	**L-2131.**
Obtain required forms from:	http://www.sctax.org/Forms+and+Instructions/2011/motorFuel/default.htm
Tax deducted from refund:	Yes.
Tax paid on separate return:	No.
Difficulty:	Moderate.
File by:	3 years from the date the fuel was purchased.
Attach documents to claim:	Attach copies of the purchase invoice. The purchaser name on the invoice must be the same as the name of the registered refund applicant. Invoices should provide the name of the purchaser, the name of the seller, the date of purchase, the gallons purchased and the price per gallon.
Send to address:	South Carolina Department of Revenue Motor Fuel Columbia, SC 29214
Don't file if:	Sales tax is more than refund.
State statute(s) supporting refund:	§ 12-28-710.
Keep records on file:	3 years.

<u>South Carolina Fuel Tax Refund Claim Instructions</u>: Fuel tax refund for gasoline purchased for farming equipment.

INSTRUCTIONS	
State the fuel is purchased in:	SC
Fuel type:	Gasoline.
Refund type:	Farming equipment.
Form name:	*Information Return for Refund of Gasoline Use in Farm Operations.*
Form #:	**L-304.**
Obtain required forms from:	http://www.sctax.org/Forms+and+Instructions/2011/motorFuel/default.htm
Tax deducted from refund:	No.
Tax paid on separate return:	No.
Difficulty:	Moderate.
File by:	3 years from the date the fuel was purchased.
Attach documents to claim:	This application must be accompanied by a true copy of the invoice.
Send to address:	South Carolina Department of Revenue Motor Fuel Columbia, SC 29214
Don't file if:	N/A.
State statute(s) supporting refund:	§ 12-28-710.
Keep records on file:	3 years.

<u>South Carolina Fuel Tax Refund Claim Instructions</u>: Fuel tax fee refund for gasoline purchased for farming equipment.

INSTRUCTIONS	
State the fuel is purchased in:	SC
Fuel type:	Gasoline.
Refund type:	Gasoline used in farm tractors or other farm equipment used in planting cultivating and harvesting.
Form name:	*Refund for Farm Gas Fee.*
Form #:	**L- 301**.
Obtain required forms from:	Call for form.
Tax deducted from refund:	http://www.sctax.org/Forms+and+Instructions/2011/ motorFuel/default.htm
Tax paid on separate return:	No.
Difficulty:	No.
File by:	Easy.
Attach documents to claim:	3 years from the date the fuel was purchased.
Send to address:	Written verification that the claim is made under penalties of perjury and lists the total amount of motor fuel subject to the user fee purchased and used for exempt purposes. The statement must show that payment for the purchase has been made and the amount of the user fee paid on the purchase has been remitted to the seller.
Don't file if:	South Carolina Department of Revenue Motor Fuel Columbia, SC 29214
State statute(s) supporting refund:	N/A.
Keep records on file:	§ 12-28-710.
State the fuel is purchased in:	3 years.

South Carolina Fuel Tax Refund Claim Instructions: Fuel tax refund for fuel purchased for off-road use and reefer trailers.

INSTRUCTIONS	
State the fuel is purchased in:	SC
Fuel type:	Undyed diesel fuel.
Refund type:	Off-road use and refrigeration (reefer) trailers.
Form name:	*Refund of Motor Fee User Fee on Diesel Used in Non-Highway Equipment.*
Form #:	**L-325.**
Obtain required forms from:	http://www.sctax.org/Forms+and+Instructions/2011/ motorFuel/default.htm
Tax deducted from refund:	Yes.
Tax paid on separate return:	No.
Difficulty:	Moderate.
File by:	3 years from the date the fuel was purchased.
Attach documents to claim:	Attach copies of invoices for the period covered that clearly show the date of purchase, the gallons purchased, the price per gallon, the name of the purchaser and the name of the seller. If you have more than one invoice, you may use up to six invoices to calculate an average price per gallon for the period covered.
Send to address:	South Carolina Department of Revenue Motor Fuel Columbia, SC 29214
Don't file if:	Sales tax is more than refund.
State statute(s) supporting refund:	N/A.
Keep records on file:	3 years.

S7outh Carolina Fuel Tax Refund Claim Instructions: Fuel tax refund for fuel purchased for PTO vehicles.

INSTRUCTIONS	
State the fuel is purchased in:	SC
Fuel type:	Gasoline, LPG (liquid petroleum gas) and undyed diesel fuel.
Refund type:	PTO (power take-off) vehicles Note: Includes Sanitation Dump Trailers, Line Trucks, Digger/Derrick, Aerial Lift Trucks, Fire Trucks, Mobile Cranes, Super Sucker, Truck Mounted/Tree Spade, Lime Spreader, Wrecker, Semi-wrecker, Car Carrier w/Hydraulic Winch, Pneumatic Tank Trucks and Refrigeration Trucks.
Form name:	*Refund of Motor Fuel User Fee Used in Trucking Equipment.*
Form #:	**L-2087.**
Obtain required forms from:	http://www.sctax.org/Forms+and+Instructions/2011/motorFuel/default.htm
Tax deducted from refund:	Yes.
Tax paid on separate return:	No.
Difficulty:	Moderate.
File by:	3 years from the date the fuel was purchased.
Attach documents to claim:	Copies of motor fuel receipts or invoices for the motor fuel used during the refund period must be attached to the application. If you have a computer generated listing the following information must be provided on the listing. Seller's name and address (city/state), the number of gallons purchased, the type of fuel and the price per gallon.
Send to address:	South Carolina Department of Revenue Motor Fuel Columbia, SC 29214
Don't file if:	Sales tax is more than refund.
State statute(s) supporting refund:	§ 12-28-710 (A)(7).
7Keep records on file:	3 years.

<u>South Carolina Fuel Tax Refund Claim Instructions</u>: Fuel tare allowance fee refund for fuel vendors with eligible purchaser status.

INSTRUCTIONS	
State the fuel is purchased in:	SC
Fuel type:	Gasoline and low sulfur undyed diesel.
Refund type:	This refund is available to fuel vendors with eligible purchaser status.
Form name:	*Tare Allowance Refund.*
Form #:	**L-2117.**
Obtain required forms from:	http://www.sctax.org/Forms+and+Instructions/2011/motorFuel/default.htm
Tax deducted from refund:	No.
Tax paid on separate return:	No.
Difficulty:	Easy.
File by:	3 years from the date the fuel was purchased.
Attach documents to claim:	Complete an eligible purchaser schedule of purchases for each month in the quarter.
Send to address:	South Carolina Department of Revenue Motor Fuel Columbia, SC 29214
Don't file if:	N/A.
State statute(s) supporting refund:	N/A.
Keep records on file:	3 years.

SOUTH DAKOTA

South Dakota Fuel Tax Refund Claim Instructions: Fuel tax refund for fuel loss.

INSTRUCTIONS	
State the fuel is purchased in:	SD
Fuel type:	Undyed diesel.
Refund type:	Contamination / Loss Note: The amount of undyed fuel accidentally mixed must exceed 500 gallons and the claimant must notify the Department of Revenue within 5 days of the accidental mixture.
Form name:	*Affidavit of Accidental Mixing of Undyed Fuel With Dyed Fuel.*
Form #:	No form number. Note: Must be notarized.
Obtain required forms from:	http://www.state.sd.us/drr2/motorvehicle/motorfuel/manual/manual.pdf
Tax deducted from refund:	Yes.
Tax paid on separate return:	No.
Difficulty:	Moderate.
File by:	The claimant must notify the Department of Revenue within 5 days of the accidental mixture.
Attach documents to claim:	Attach copies of all fuel invoices related to this accidental mixture.
Send to address:	South Dakota Department of Revenue 445 East Capitol Ave. Pierre, SD 57501
Don't file if:	The amount of undyed fuel accidentally mixed is less than 500 gallons or if sales tax is greater than refund.
State statute(s) supporting refund:	SDCL § 10-47B-132.
Keep records on file:	3 years.

<u>South Dakota Fuel Tax Refund Claim Instructions</u>: Fuel tax refund for retailers of fuel sold to customers where the amount due is uncollected as bad debt.

INSTRUCTIONS	
State the fuel is purchased in:	SD
Fuel type:	Gasoline, gasohol, undyed diesel fuel or LPG (liquefied petroleum gas).
Refund type:	Any licensed wholesaler or retailer may apply for a refund of fuel taxes paid on fuel sold to a customer whose account is found to be worthless. An account is considered worthless when it has been claimed as uncollectible and deducted as an expense on the seller's Federal income tax return.
Form name:	*Affidavit for Bad Debt Loss – Marketer.*
Form #:	No Form Number.
Obtain required forms from:	http://www.state.sd.us/drr2/motorvehicle/motorfuel/manual/manual.pdf
Tax deducted from refund:	No.
Tax paid on separate return:	No.
Difficulty:	Moderate.
File by:	No further tax refunds will be paid to suppliers or marketers who sell fuel to this customer for a three-year period
Attach documents to claim:	To qualify for this refund, the marketer must provide the Department with sufficient written evidence to justify the claim and to enable the Department to collect payment from the delinquent customer. Include copy of Federal income tax return.
Send to address:	South Dakota Department of Revenue 445 East Capitol Ave. Pierre, SD 57501
Don't file if:	N/A.
State statute(s) supporting refund:	SDCL § 10-47B-134.
Keep records on file:	3 years.

South Dakota Fuel Tax Refund Claim Instructions: Fuel tax refund for suppliers of fuel sold to customers where amount due is uncollected as bad debt.

INSTRUCTIONS	
State the fuel is purchased in:	SD
Fuel type:	Gasoline, gasohol and undyed diesel fuel.
Refund type:	Any licensed supplier may apply for a refund of fuel taxes paid on gasoline, gasohol, and undyed diesel fuel sold to a customer who fails to remit payment for such fuel. However, a supplier may collect this refund for a specific customer only once every three years. After submitting this affidavit, the supplier becomes responsible for fuel taxes due on future sales to the same customer.
Form name:	*Affidavit for Bad Debt Loss – Supplier.*
Form #:	No Form number.
Obtain required forms from:	http://www.state.sd.us/drr2/motorvehicle/motorfuel/manual/manual.pdf
Tax deducted from refund:	No.
Tax paid on separate return:	No.
Difficulty:	Moderate.
File by:	No further tax refunds will be paid to suppliers or marketers who sell fuel to this customer for a three-year period
Attach documents to claim:	To qualify for this refund, the supplier must provide the Department with sufficient written evidence to justify the claim and to enable the Department to collect payment from the delinquent customer.
Send to address:	South Dakota Department of Revenue 445 East Capitol Ave. Pierre, SD 57501
Don't file if:	N/A.
State statute(s) supporting refund:	SDCL § 10-47B-133.
Keep records on file:	3 years.

<u>South Dakota Fuel Tax Refund Claim Instructions</u>: Fuel tax refund for fuel loss.

INSTRUCTIONS	
State the fuel is purchased in:	SD
Fuel type:	Gasoline, gasohol and undyed diesel fuel.
Refund type:	Any person or business licensed in the sale of fuels may collect a refund of fuel taxes paid on fuel lost by leakage or theft, or fuel lost or destroyed by fire, flood, tornado, windstorm or explosion.
Form name:	*Affidavit of Loss of Taxable Fuel.*
Form #:	No form number. Note: must be notarized.
Obtain required forms from:	http://www.state.sd.us/drr2/motorvehicle/motorfuel/manual/manual.pdf
Tax deducted from refund:	No.
Tax paid on separate return:	No.
Difficulty:	Moderate.
File by:	All claims must be filed with the Department of Revenue within 30 days after the loss is discovered.
Attach documents to claim:	Police and insurance reports.
Send to address:	South Dakota Department of Revenue 445 East Capitol Ave. Pierre, SD 57501
Don't file if:	• For a refund of taxes on fuel lost by leakage or theft, the total gallon is less than 501 gallons. • For a refund of taxes on fuel lost or destroyed by fire, flood, tornado, windstorm or explosion, the total gallons is less than 101 gallons.
State statute(s) supporting refund:	SDCL § 10-47B-123, 10-47B-137.
Keep records on file:	3 years.

South Dakota Fuel Tax Refund Claim Instructions: Fuel tax refund for undyed diesel used for heating purposes.

INSTRUCTIONS	
State the fuel is purchased in:	SD
Fuel type:	Undyed diesel fuel.
Refund type:	Heating. Note: In the event that a customer is unable to purchase dyed diesel fuel for use as heating oil, a marketer or retailer may sell undyed diesel fuel in its place. The marketer or retailer must then testify through affidavit that he or she was unable to obtain dyed diesel fuel and had to substitute undyed diesel fuel. With this affidavit, the customer can then apply for a refund of fuel taxes, but must pay sales tax on the cost of the fuel minus fuel tax.
Form name:	*Affidavit of Sale of Undyed Diesel Fuel As Heating Oil.*
Form #:	No form number. Must be notarized.
Obtain required forms from:	http://www.state.sd.us/drr2/motorvehicle/motorfuel/manual/manual.pdf
Tax deducted from refund:	Yes.
Tax paid on separate return:	No.
Difficulty:	Moderate.
File by:	No further tax refunds will be paid to suppliers or marketers who sell fuel to this customer for a three-year period.
Attach documents to claim:	Attach a copy of the original sales invoice. The claimant shall submit a sworn affidavit from the retail dealer testifying that the dealer had tried to obtain dyed heating oil from the dealer's regular sources but was unable to obtain the fuel because no dyed heating fuel was available.
Send to address:	South Dakota Department of Revenue 445 East Capitol Ave. Pierre, SD 57501
Don't file if:	Sales tax is greater than refund.
State statute(s) supporting refund:	Reference SDCL 10-47B-128.
Keep records on file:	3 years.

<u>South Dakota Fuel Tax Refund Claim Instructions</u>: Fuel tax refund for producers of biodiesel.

INSTRUCTIONS	
State the fuel is purchased in:	SD
Fuel type:	Biodiesel sold to purchasers.
Refund type:	Biodiesel producers may obtain a refund of the taxes paid for ethanol and/or methanol that is used in the production of biodiesel. This refund can be claimed on the *Biodiesel Producer Tax Return*.
Form name:	*Biodiesel Producer Return.*
Form #:	**DOR/DMV FORM 592**
Obtain required forms from:	http://www.state.sd.us/drr2/motorvehicle/motorfuel/manual/manual.pdf
Tax deducted from refund:	Yes.
Tax paid on separate return:	No.
Difficulty:	Moderate.
File by:	No further tax refunds will be paid to suppliers or marketers who sell fuel to this customer for a three-year period.
Attach documents to claim:	Attach a copy of the original sales invoice. The claimant shall submit a sworn affidavit from the retail dealer testifying that the dealer had tried to obtain dyed heating oil from the dealer's regular sources but was unable to obtain the fuel because no dyed heating fuel was available.
Send to address:	Mail Remittance Center P.O. Box 5055 Sioux Falls, SD 57117-5055
Don't file if:	N/A.
State statute(s) supporting refund:	10-47B-120.1.
Keep records on file:	3 years.

South Dakota Fuel Tax Refund Claim Instructions: Fuel tax refund for fuel sold by ethanol producers in the denaturing process.

INSTRUCTIONS	
State the fuel is purchased in:	SD
Fuel type:	Gasoline and/or natural gasoline used as a denaturant.
Refund type:	Ethanol producers may obtain a refund of the taxes paid for natural gasoline and/or gasoline that is used to denature alcohol. This refund can be claimed on the *Ethanol Producer Return*.
Form name:	*Ethanol Producer Return.*
Form #:	**DOR/DMV Form 592**.
Obtain required forms from:	http://www.state.sd.us/drr2/motorvehicle/motorfuel/manual/manual.pdf
Tax deducted from refund:	Yes.
Tax paid on separate return:	No.
Difficulty:	Moderate.
File by:	No further tax refunds will be paid to suppliers or marketers who sell fuel to this customer for a three-year period.
Attach documents to claim:	Attach a copy of the original sales invoice. The claimant shall submit a sworn affidavit from the retail dealer testifying that the dealer had tried to obtain dyed heating oil from the dealer's regular sources but was unable to obtain the fuel because no dyed heating fuel was available.
Send to address:	Mail Remittance Center P.O. Box 5055 Sioux Falls, SD 57117-5055
Don't file if:	N/A.
State statute(s) supporting refund:	10-47B-120.
Keep records on file:	3 years.

<u>South Dakota Fuel Tax Refund Claim Instructions</u>: Fuel tax refund for fuel exports and diversions.

INSTRUCTIONS	
State the fuel is purchased in:	SD
Fuel type:	Gasoline, other /natural, 100% methyl alcohol, undyed biodiesel blend, dyed biodiesel blend, jet fuel, undyed diesel & kerosene, dyed diesel & kerosene, AVGAS, 100% ethyl alcohol.
Refund type:	A licensed Importer/Exporter may apply for and obtain a refund for taxes paid to this state on motor fuel and undyed special fuel under the following conditions: • Fuel which was loaded at a bulk plant in this state and exported; • Fuel that is loaded at a terminal in this state indicating South Dakota as the destination state and then diverted to another state; • Fuel that is withdrawn from an out-of-state terminal, and purchased from a licensed Supplier, with a South Dakota destination, and is then diverted to another state; and • Fuel purchased from a licensed Supplier indicating South Dakota as the destination state and then diverted to another state.
Form name:	*South Dakota Importer and Exporter Tax Return.*
Form #:	**MV-594**.
Obtain required forms from:	http://www.state.sd.us/drr2/motorvehicle/motorfuel/manual/manual.pdf
Tax deducted from refund:	Yes.
Tax paid on separate return:	No.
Difficulty:	Moderate.
File by:	No further tax refunds will be paid to suppliers or marketers who sell fuel to this customer for a three-year period.
Attach documents to claim:	The claimant shall submit a copy of the original bill of lading, and a copy of the diversion.
Send to address:	Mail Remittance Center P.O. Box 5055 Sioux Falls, SD 57117-5055
Don't file if:	N/A.
State statute(s) supporting refund:	10-47B-125.
Keep records on file:	3 years.

<u>South Dakota Fuel Tax Refund Claim Instructions</u>: Fuel tax refund for fuel exports and diversions.

INSTRUCTIONS	
State the fuel is purchased in:	SD
Fuel type:	Gasoline, 100% ethyl alcohol, AVGAS, undyed diesel fuel, jet fuel, 100% methyl alcohol and undyed biodiesel.
Refund type:	Gallons of fuel sold in bulk to: • A location on a licensed Indian school's premises. The school must be licensed by the Department of Revenue to purchase fuel exempt from state taxation. List school names and license numbers on refund. • Native American tribes. • Federal government agencies.
Form name:	*Marketer Refund.*
Form #:	**DOR/DMV FORM 573.**
Obtain required forms from:	http://www.state.sd.us/drr2/motorvehicle/motorfuel/manual/manual.pdf
Tax deducted from refund:	No.
Tax paid on separate return:	No.
Difficulty:	Moderate.
File by:	Refunds are limited to a period within 15 months of transaction date.
Attach documents to claim:	No further tax refunds will be paid to suppliers or marketers who sell fuel to this customer for a three-year period.
Send to address:	Mail Remittance Center P.O. Box 5055 Sioux Falls, SD 57117-5055
Don't file if:	The school is not licensed by the Department of Revenue to purchase fuel exempt from state taxation. List school names and license numbers with refund claim.
State statute(s) supporting refund:	10-47B-122.
Keep records on file:	3 years.

South Dakota Fuel Tax Refund Claim Instructions: Fuel tax refund for fuel purchased by Native Americans.

INSTRUCTIONS	
State the fuel is purchased in:	SD
Fuel type:	Gasoline, undyed clear diesel, gasohol (ethanol blend), LPG, clear soy diesel, AVGAS, jet fuel, E85, M85, CNG and other fuels.
Refund type:	A tribal member who has purchased motor fuel or special fuel in Indian country may apply for a refund of the fuel tax paid.
Form name:	*Motor Fuel Tax Tribal Refund Application - Pourier v. DOR.*
Form #:	**MF-003.**
Obtain required forms from:	https://www.state.sd.us/eforms/secure/eforms/non1822V1-MotorFuelTaxTribalRefundApplication.pdf
Tax deducted from refund:	No.
Tax paid on separate return:	No.
Difficulty:	Moderate.
File by:	To be eligible, the individual must be an enrolled tribal member and have purchased the fuel within the last 15months on Indian country controlled by their own tribe.
Attach documents to claim:	Copies of invoices or receipts, or any other evidence substantiating claim.
Send to address:	South Dakota Department of Revenue 445 East Capitol Ave. Pierre, SD 57501
Don't file if:	N/A.
State statute(s) supporting refund:	N/A.
Keep records on file:	3 years.

TENNESSEE

Tennessee Fuel Tax Refund Claim Instructions: Fuel tax refund for fuel purchased for reefer trailers and PTO equipment.

INSTRUCTIONS	
State the fuel is purchased in:	TN
Fuel type:	Gasoline and undyed diesel fuel.
Refund type:	Construction Equipment, PTO (power take-off) vehicles and refrigeration (reefer) trailers. Construction and PTO equipment includes: concrete mixers, pumpers, pneumatic & boom unloaders, mobile self-propelled rock drills and pump unloaders.
Form name:	*TN Department of Revenue Specialized Equipment Claim for Refund.*
Form #:	**PET 354.**
Obtain required forms from:	http://www.tn.gov/revenue/forms/petro/index.shtml
Tax deducted from refund:	No.
Tax paid on separate return:	No.
Difficulty:	Difficult.
File by:	If claim is for January-June (90 days following the end of June). If claim is for July-December (90 days following the end of December).
Attach documents to claim:	Copies of motor fuel receipts or invoices.
Send to address:	Tennessee Department of Revenue Andrew Jackson Building 500 Deaderick Street Nashville, TN 37242
Don't file if:	Claim is under $50.00.
State statute(s) supporting refund:	Tenn. Code Ann. § 67-3-414.
Keep records on file:	5 years.

<u>Tennessee Fuel Tax Refund Claim Instructions</u>: Fuel tax refund for fuel used purchased for farming equipment.

INSTRUCTIONS	
State the fuel is purchased in:	TN
Fuel type:	Gasoline.
Refund type:	Farming equipment.
Form name:	*Agricultural Purposes Claim for Refund.*
Form #:	**PET 353**.
Obtain required forms from:	http://www.tn.gov/revenue/forms/petro/index.shtml
Tax deducted from refund:	No.
Tax paid on separate return:	No.
Difficulty:	Difficult.
File by:	Semiannual claim: Must be filed on or before April 15 and October 15 following the end of each semiannual period ending on the immediately preceding December 31 and June 30 periods respectively. Annual claim: On April 15 of the following year if filed annually.
Attach documents to claim:	Copies of motor fuel receipts or invoices.
Send to address:	Tennessee Department of Revenue Andrew Jackson Building 500 Deaderick Street Nashville, TN 37242
Don't file if:	Claim is under $25.00.
State statute(s) supporting refund:	Tenn. Code Ann. § 67-3-411.
Keep records on file:	5 years.

Tennessee Fuel Tax Refund Claim Instructions: Fuel tax refund for fuel affected by contamination / loss.

INSTRUCTIONS	
State the fuel is purchased in:	TN
Fuel type:	Gasoline and undyed diesel fuel.
Refund type:	Contamination / Loss. Note: Wholesalers who have sold fuel to prepaid users, limited use users, contaminated fuel, casualty loss.
Form name:	*Wholesaler Application for Refund.*
Form #:	**PET 375.**
Obtain required forms from:	http://www.tn.gov/revenue/forms/petro/index.shtml
Tax deducted from refund:	No.
Tax paid on separate return:	No.
Difficulty:	Difficult.
File by:	Loss must be reported to the commissioner within 3 business days of the date of the loss, except that losses not exceeding one thousand gallons (1,000 gals.) need not be reported. With respect to all losses, the vendor shall file with the commissioner a written claim and statement explaining the occurrence of the loss within 60 days of the time of loss.
Attach documents to claim:	Copies of motor fuel receipts or invoices.
Send to address:	Tennessee Department of Revenue Andrew Jackson Building 500 Deaderick Street Nashville, TN 37242
Don't file if:	N/A.
State statute(s) supporting refund:	Tenn. Code Ann. § 67-3-415 (contaminated fuels). Tenn. Code Ann. § 67-3-416 (casualty loss).
Keep records on file:	5 years.

Tennessee Fuel Tax Refund Claim Instructions: Fuel tax refund for diesel purchased for boats, farming, golf-course equipment, heating, fabrication equipment, logging, mining, off-road usage, oilfield equipment, snowmobiles and stationary equipment.

INSTRUCTIONS	
State the fuel is purchased in:	TN
Fuel type:	Undyed diesel fuel.
Refund type:	Boats (off-road refund), fabrication, golf course equipment (off-road refund), heating, logging (off-road refund), mining (off-road refund), off-road vehicles, oilfield equipment (off-road refund), snowmobiles (off-road refund) and stationary equipment (off-road refund).
Form name:	*End User Claim for Refund.*
Form #:	**PET 371.**
Obtain required forms from:	http://www.tn.gov/revenue/forms/petro/index.shtml
Tax deducted from refund:	Yes, sales and use tax is due upon receipt of refund.
Tax paid on separate return:	Yes.
Difficulty:	Difficult.
File by:	1 year from the date of the last purchase represented in the claim.
Attach documents to claim:	Copies of motor fuel receipts or invoices.
Send to address:	Tennessee Department of Revenue Andrew Jackson Building 500 Deaderick Street Nashville, TN 37242
Don't file if:	Claim Is for less than $250. Note: If less than $250.00, attach this completed report to subsequent claim (up to 2 years) until total claim exceeds $250.00.
State statute(s) supporting refund:	Tenn. Code Ann. § 67-3-417 (Fabrication). Tenn. Code Ann. § 67-3-418 (off-road).
Keep records on file:	5 years.

Tennessee Fuel Tax Refund Claim Instructions: Fuel tax refund for fuel purchased for fire trucks, public utility-owned equipment school-owned equipment and government-owned vehicles.

INSTRUCTIONS	
State the fuel is purchased in:	TN
Fuel type:	Gasoline and undyed diesel.
Refund type:	Charities, fire departments, public utilities, schools, state and Federal government agencies. Notes: Must hold an exemption permit issued by the commissioner. Charities, fire departments, public utilities and schools must hold a government agency permit.
Form name:	*Governmental Sales Claim for Refund.*
Form #:	**PET 357.**
Obtain required forms from:	http://www.tn.gov/revenue/forms/petro/index.shtml
Tax deducted from refund:	No.
Tax paid on separate return:	No.
Difficulty:	Moderate.
File by:	One omnibus claim may be filed after January 1 and before April 1 for any exempt sales made during the previous calendar year for which a claim has not been made.
Attach documents to claim:	Copies of all invoices for sales on which the licensee is applying for refund or claiming a credit. The invoices submitted with any such application shall each contain the exemption permit number for the governmental agency to which the sales were made.
Send to address:	Tennessee Department of Revenue Andrew Jackson Building 500 Deaderick Street Nashville, TN 37242
Don't file if:	Licensed wholesalers, importers or suppliers shall not be entitled to a refund on sales made to any person who does not hold a valid governmental agency exemption permit at the time of such sale.
State statute(s) supporting refund:	Tenn. Code Ann. § 67-3-413.
Keep records on file:	5 years.

<u>Tennessee Fuel Tax Refund Claim Instructions</u>: Fuel tax refund for fuel exports sold by unlicensed exporters.

INSTRUCTIONS	
State the fuel is purchased in:	TN
Fuel type:	Gasoline, jet fuel, aviation gas, kerosene, undyed diesel.
Refund type:	Exports. Notes: Unlicensed exporters may request a refund only on Tennessee tax paid gallons exported by transport truck or tank wagon.
Form name:	*Unlicensed Exporter Claim for Refund.*
Form #:	**PET 380**.
Obtain required forms from:	http://www.tn.gov/revenue/forms/petro/index.shtml
Tax deducted from refund:	No.
Tax paid on separate return:	No.
Difficulty:	Difficult.
File by:	A claim for refund must be filed within 3 years from December 31st of the year when the shipment was exported.
Attach documents to claim:	If filing Schedule B, Copies of motor fuel receipts or invoices and shipping papers.
Send to address:	Tennessee Department of Revenue Andrew Jackson Building 500 Deaderick Street Nashville, TN 37242
Don't file if:	N/A.
State statute(s) supporting refund:	Tenn. Code Ann. § 67-3-412.
Keep records on file:	5 years.

Tennessee Fuel Tax Refund Claim Instructions: Fuel tax refund for fuel exports sold by licensed exporters.

INSTRUCTIONS	
State the fuel is purchased in:	TN
Fuel type:	Gasoline, jet fuel, aviation gas, kerosene, undyed diesel.
Refund type:	Exports. Notes: Licensed Exporters may request a refund only on Tennessee tax paid gallons exported by transport truck or tank wagon.
Form name:	*Tennessee Department of Revenue Exporter Tax Return & Claim for Refund.*
Form #:	**PET 377**.
Obtain required forms from:	http://www.tn.gov/revenue/forms/petro/index.shtml
Tax deducted from refund:	No.
Tax paid on separate return:	No.
Difficulty:	Difficult.
File by:	A claim for refund must be filed within 3 years from December 31st of the year when the shipment was exported.
Attach documents to claim:	To claim a refund under this part, a person must present to the department a statement that contains a written verification that the claim is made under penalty of perjury and lists the total amount of taxable petroleum products subject to refund.
Send to address:	Tennessee Department of Revenue Andrew Jackson Building 500 Deaderick Street Nashville, TN 37242
Don't file if:	N/A.
State statute(s) supporting refund:	Tenn. Code Ann. § 67-3-412.
Keep records on file:	5 years.

TEXAS

Texas Fuel Tax Refund Claim Instructions: Fuel tax refund for fuel affected by contamination and used in incidental highway travel. Further refund allowances include fuel purchased for government-owned vehicles, non-profits, off-road use, schools, PTO vehicles, the volunteer fire department and other forms of qualified usage.

INSTRUCTIONS	
State the fuel is purchased in:	TX
Fuel type:	Gasoline and undyed diesel fuel.
Refund type:	**Gasoline**: CTC (commercial transportation company), contamination / loss, exports, incidental highway travel (4mpg), MTA (metropolitan transit authority), nonprofit electric, off-road, PTO (power take-off equipment), schools, telephone cooperative, state and Federal government agencies and volunteer fire department. **Undyed Diesel**: Manufacturing feedstock, removal of drill cuttings in oil and gas production, oil field well servicing, exports, qualified passenger motor vehicles, state and Federal government agencies, contamination / loss, schools, MTA (metropolitan transit authority), non-profit electric, telephone cooperative and volunteer fire department.
Form name:	*Texas Claim for Refund of Gasoline or Diesel Fuel Taxes.*
Form #:	**06-106**.
Obtain required forms from:	http://www.window.state.tx.us/taxinfo/taxforms/06-forms.html
Tax deducted from refund:	No, however, the refund will be paid less a 2% fee For refunds for buses, the refund will be paid less 25%.
Tax paid on separate return:	No.
Difficulty:	Moderate.
File by:	1 year from purchase or use of it withdrawn for own use. 4 years for overpayment.
Attach documents to claim:	Copies of motor fuel receipts or invoices, equipment lists and distribution logs. These documents must be available upon request.
Send to address:	Comptroller of Public Accounts 111 E. 17th Street Austin, Texas 78774
Don't file if:	Claim is for less than 100 gallons.
State statute(s) supporting refund:	Rule §3.432.
Keep records on file:	4 years.

UTAH

<u>Utah Fuel Tax Refund Claim Instructions</u>: Fuel tax refund for fuel purchased for farming, non-licensed suppliers, Native American-owned vehicles, government-owned vehicles and planes. Further refund allowances include fuel affected by contamination / loss, returns to refinery and payments uncollected due to bankruptcy.

INSTRUCTIONS	
State the fuel is purchased in:	UT
Fuel type:	CNG (compressed natural gas), gasoline, jet fuel, and undyed diesel fuel.
Refund type:	Contamination / loss (By Fire, Floods, Crime, Accident), discharged from bankruptcy, exports (from non-licensed suppliers), farming equipment (Non Profit), Native American, planes, returns to refinery for refining and state and Federal government agencies.
Form name:	*Utah Application for Fuel Tax Refund.*
Form #:	**TC-116**.
Obtain required forms from:	http://tax.utah.gov/forms/currentforms
Tax deducted from refund:	No.
Tax paid on separate return:	No.
Difficulty:	Moderate.
File by:	3 years from the date the fuel was purchased.
Attach documents to claim:	Copies of motor fuel receipts or invoices or bulk disbursement tickets which identify the equipment into which the fuel was placed.
Send to address:	Utah State Tax Commission 210 N 1950 W Salt Lake City, Utah 84134
Don't file if:	N/A.
State statute(s) supporting refund:	§ 59-13-201.
Keep records on file:	5 years.

<u>Utah Fuel Tax Refund Claim Instructions</u>: Fuel tax refund for fuel purchased for PTO vehicles and reefer trailers.

INSTRUCTIONS	
State the fuel is purchased in:	UT
Fuel type:	Undyed diesel fuel.
Refund type:	PTO (power take-off) vehicles and refrigeration (reefer) trailers.
Form name:	*Application For Undyed Diesel Fuel Tax Refund.*
Form #:	**TC-942** (This form is for Utah based carriers only. Use form TC-922, if SFU account)
Obtain required forms from:	http://tax.utah.gov/forms/currentforms
Tax deducted from refund:	Yes.
Tax paid on separate return:	No.
Difficulty:	Difficult.
File by:	3 years from the date the fuel was purchased.
Attach documents to claim:	Documentation should include fuel purchase invoices (or bulk disbursement tickets) which identify the equipment into which the fuel was placed.
Send to address:	Utah State Tax Commission 210 N 1950 W Salt Lake City, Utah 84134
Don't file if:	Sales tax is greater than refund.
State statute(s) supporting refund:	§ 59-13-201.
Keep records on file:	5 years.

VIRGINIA

Virginia Fuel Tax Refund Claim Instructions: Fuel tax refund for fuel purchased for ATV's, construction equipment, farming equipment, fire trucks, government-owned vehicles, lawn equipment, non-profit transportation vehicles, off-road, planes, PTO vehicles, racing vehicles, reefer trailers, school buses, stationary equipment, volunteer rescue squads and well drillers. Further refund allowances include fuel contamination / loss.

INSTRUCTIONS	
State the fuel is purchased in:	VA
Fuel type:	Gasoline and undyed diesel fuel.
Refund type:	ATVs (all-terrain vehicles), construction equipment, farming equipment, fire department, lawn equipment, contamination/loss, off-road use, planes, PTO (power take-off equipment), racing, refrigeration (reefer) trailers, school buses, state or Federal government, stationary engines, trains, volunteer rescue squads and well drillers. Other: Vehicles owned by a non-profit organization providing specialized transportation for the elderly and disabled.
Form name:	*Fuels Tax Refund Application.*
Form #:	**TS 216**.
Obtain required forms from:	http://www.dmv.state.va.us/webdoc/citizen/fuel_tax.asp
Tax deducted from refund:	No.
Tax paid on separate return:	No.
Difficulty:	Moderate.
File by:	1 year from the date on the Invoice showing the fuel purchase.
Attach documents to claim:	Original motor fuel receipts or invoices. Claims supported by copies of receipts and receipts marked "Duplicate" are not eligible for a refund. Invoices must show the exact date of purchase , the number of gallons and type of fuel purchased, the amount paid for the fuel, the seller's name and location, be readable, and in date order.
Send to address:	Department of Motor Vehicles Tax Services Refund Section P. O. Box 27422 Richmond, Virginia 23261
Don't file if:	Claim is for less than 5 gallons.
State statute(s) supporting refund:	§ 58.1-2259.
Keep records on file:	4 years.

<u>Virginia Fuel Tax Refund Claim Instructions</u>: Fuel tax refund for fuel used purchased for boats and commercial fishing.

INSTRUCTIONS	
State the fuel is purchased in:	VA
Fuel type:	Gasoline and undyed diesel fuel.
Refund type:	Boating and commercial fishing.
Form name:	*Fuels Tax Refund Application For Fuel Used in Boats or Watercraft*.
Form #:	**TS 217**.
Obtain required forms from:	http://www.dmv.state.va.us/webdoc/citizen/fuel_tax.asp
Tax deducted from refund:	No.
Tax paid on separate return:	No.
Difficulty:	Moderate.
File by:	1 year from the date on the Invoice showing the fuel purchase.
Attach documents to claim:	Original motor fuel receipts or invoices. Claims supported by copies of receipts and receipts marked "Duplicate" are not eligible for a refund.
Send to address:	Department of Motor Vehicles Tax Services Refund Section P. O. Box 27422 Richmond, Virginia 23261
Don't file if:	Claim is for less than 5 gallons.
State statute(s) supporting refund:	§ 58.1-2259.
Keep records on file:	4 years.

<u>Virginia Fuel Tax Refund Claim Instructions</u>: Fuel tax refund for fuel exports.

INSTRUCTIONS	
State the fuel is purchased in:	VA
Fuel type:	Gasoline, jet fuel and undyed diesel fuel.
Refund type:	Exports.
Form name:	*Fuels Tax Refund Application - Exports.*
Form #:	**TS 219.**
Obtain required forms from:	http://www.dmv.state.va.us/webdoc/citizen/fuel_tax.asp
Tax deducted from refund:	No.
Tax paid on separate return:	No.
Difficulty:	Moderate.
File by:	1 year from the date on the Invoice showing the fuel purchase.
Attach documents to claim:	Original motor fuel receipts or invoices. Claims supported by copies of receipts and receipts marked "Duplicate" are not eligible for a refund.
Send to address:	Department of Motor Vehicles Tax Services Refund Section P. O. Box 27422 Richmond, Virginia 23261
Don't file if:	Claim is for less than 5 gallons.
State statute(s) supporting refund:	§ 58.1-2259.
Keep records on file:	4 years.

Virginia Fuel Tax Refund Claim Instructions: Fuel tax refund for fuel purchased for taxis.

INSTRUCTIONS	
State the fuel is purchased in:	VA
Fuel type:	Gasoline and undyed diesel fuel.
Refund type:	Taxis.
Form name:	*Fuels Tax Refund Application Used in Tax Operation.*
Form #:	**TS 221**.
Obtain required forms from:	http://www.dmv.state.va.us/webdoc/citizen/fuel_tax.asp
Tax deducted from refund:	No.
Tax paid on separate return:	No.
Difficulty:	Moderate.
File by:	1 year from the date on the Invoice showing the fuel purchase.
Attach documents to claim:	Original motor fuel receipts or invoices. Claims supported by copies of receipts and receipts marked "Duplicate" are not eligible for a refund.
Send to address:	Department of Motor Vehicles Tax Services Refund Section P. O. Box 27422 Richmond, Virginia 23261
Don't file if:	Claim is for less than 5 gallons.
State statute(s) supporting refund:	§ 58.1-2259.
Keep records on file:	4 years.

Virginia Fuel Tax Refund Claim Instructions: Fuel tax refund for fuel purchased for common carriers.

INSTRUCTIONS	
State the fuel is purchased in:	VA
Fuel type:	Gasoline and undyed diesel fuel.
Refund type:	Common Carriers. Note: Refunds are granted only to regular route common carriers of passengers that hold a valid regular route common carrier operating authority certificate issued by the DMV.
Form name:	*Fuels Tax Refund Application Regular Route Common Carrier of Passengers.*
Form #:	**TS 225**.
Obtain required forms from:	http://www.dmv.state.va.us/webdoc/citizen/fuel_tax.asp
Tax deducted from refund:	No.
Tax paid on separate return:	No.
Difficulty:	Moderate.
File by:	1 year from the date on the Invoice showing the fuel purchase.
Attach documents to claim:	Original motor fuel receipts or invoices. Claims supported by copies of receipts and receipts marked "Duplicate" are not eligible for a refund.
Send to address:	Department of Motor Vehicles Tax Services Refund Section P. O. Box 27422 Richmond, Virginia 23261
Don't file if:	Claim is for less than 5 gallons.
State statute(s) supporting refund:	§ 58.1-2259.
Keep records on file:	4 years.

VERMONT

Vermont Fuel Tax Refund Claim Instructions: Fuel tax refund for fuel purchased for farming equipment, fire trucks, government-owned vehicles, heating, logging, non-profit public transit system buses, off-road use, PTO vehicles, reefer trailers, school buses, stationary equipment and unlicensed vehicles.

INSTRUCTIONS	
State the fuel is purchased in:	VT
Fuel type:	Undyed diesel fuel.
Refund type:	Farming equipment, fire department, furnaces, any device used to heat a building or structure, logging, non-profit public transit system, off-road, refrigeration (reefer) trailers, PTO (power take-off) vehicles, school district, state and Federal government agencies, stationary equipment, unlicensed equipment & vehicles.
Form name:	*Diesel Tax Refund Application.*
Form #:	**TA-VP-35**.
Obtain required forms from:	http://dmv.vermont.gov/commercial_trucking/fuel_tax_refunds
Tax deducted from refund:	Yes, in most cases the gallons allowed for diesel credit are subject to Vermont sales and use tax at 6% of the cost of fuel (including tax).
Tax paid on separate return:	Yes.
Difficulty:	Easy.
File by:	33 months following the due date of the report covering the reporting period in which the purchase was made.
Attach documents to claim:	Copies of motor fuel receipts or invoices indicating the state tax and Motor Fuel Transportation Infrastructure Assessment fee were paid. IFTA returns required if claim is for non-taxable purpose of IFTA vehicles.
Send to address:	VT Department of Motor Vehicles 120 State St. Montpelier, VT 05603
Don't file if:	N/A.
State statute(s) supporting refund:	V.S.A. § 23-27-3020.
Keep records on file:	4 years.

WASHINGTON

Washington Fuel Tax Refund Claim Instructions: Fuel tax refund for fuel purchased for boats, construction, emergency medical air transport, farming, industrial usage, lawn equipment, off-road use, planes, reefer trailers and government-owned vehicles.

INSTRUCTIONS	
State the fuel is purchased in:	WA
Fuel type:	Aviation gas, biodiesel, gasoline, ethanol, jet fuel, propane and undyed diesel fuel.
Refund type:	Boating, construction equipment, emergency medical air transport, farming equipment, industrial equipment, lawn equipment, off-road use, refrigeration (reefer) trailers, state and Federal government agencies.
Form name:	*Fuel Tax Refund Permit Application.*
Form #:	**FT-442-071.** After application is received, Fuel Tax Refund Claim form with instructions will be sent. Fill out the claim form and return it with your fuel invoices.
Obtain required forms from:	http://www.dol.wa.gov/vehicleregistration/ftrefunds.html
Tax deducted from refund:	Yes.
Tax paid on separate return:	No.
Difficulty:	Moderate.
File by:	13 months from the date the fuel was purchased. The fuel invoices must be dated within 13 months of the postmark date of the refund claim.
Attach documents to claim:	Copies of motor fuel receipts or invoices.
Send to address:	Fuel Tax Refund Unit Department of Licensing P.O. Box 9228 Olympia, WA 98507
Don't file if:	Less than 54 gallons were purchased or sold in the past 13 months.
State statute(s) supporting refund:	RCWs § 82.36.280, 82.38.080, 82.42.030.
Keep records on file:	5 years.

WEST VIRGINIA

<u>West Virginia Fuel Tax Refund Claim Instructions</u>: Fuel tax refund for fuel purchased for farming, government-owned vehicles, off-road use, poultry house usage, PTO vehicles and reefer trailers.

INSTRUCTIONS	
State the fuel is purchased in:	WV
Fuel type:	Biodiesel, clear kerosene, gasoline, heating oil, propane and undyed diesel fuel.
Refund type:	Casualty/loss, evaporation, farming, kerosene for heating purposes, off-road use, propane sold to poultry houses, fuel overpayment, PTO (power take-off) vehicles, state and Federal government agencies and refrigeration (reefer) trailers.
Form name:	Various, see below.
Form #:	Required form(s): **WV/MFR-14**, *West Virginia Motor Fuel Tax Refund Application.* Additional forms required based on fuel or refund type: **Schedule A**, *Sellers of Propane to Poultry House Consumers.* **Schedule B**, *Casualty Loss Statement for Lost Fuel.* **Schedule C**, *Retailers of Clear Kerosene – 637-UP.* **Schedule D**, *Refund Worksheet (Gasoline/Special Fuel.* **Schedule E**, *Retail Evaporation.*
Obtain required forms from:	http://www.wva.state.wv.us/wvtax/motorFuelInformationAndForms.aspx
Tax deducted from refund:	No.
Tax paid on separate return:	No.
Difficulty:	Moderate.
File by:	**Agriculture equipment** - 12 months from the month the fuel was purchased. **Casualty/Loss, Evaporation, Poultry House** - 3 years from the month the fuel was purchased. **Off-road, PTO, Reefer Trailers** - 30 days from the month the fuel was purchased. **State and Federal government agencies** - The 31st day of August for fuel purchases made during the prior year ending June 30th.
Attach documents to claim:	In lieu of purchase receipts submit invoice summary schedule.
Send to address:	WV State Tax Department Tax Account Administration Division P.O. Box 2991 Charleston, WV 25330
Don't file if:	Less than 25 gallons were purchased for agriculture, off-road or PTO usage.
State statute(s) supporting refund:	§11-14-5.
Keep records on file:	3 years.

WISCONSIN

Wisconsin Fuel Tax Refund Claim Instructions: Fuel tax refund for fuel purchased for farming, construction equipment, logging, off-road vehicles, PTO vehicles, reefer trailers, taxis and unlicensed vehicles.

INSTRUCTIONS	
State the fuel is purchased in:	WI
Fuel type:	Gasoline, gasohol, CNG (Compressed Natural Gas), LPG (Liquid Petroleum Gas) and undyed diesel fuel.
Refund type:	ATVs (all-terrain vehicles) registered for private use, construction equipment, farming, logging, off-road, PTO (power take-off) vehicles, refrigeration (reefer) trailers, taxis and unlicensed vehicles.
Form name:	*Fuel Tax Refund Claim.*
Form #:	**MF-001**.
Obtain required forms from:	http://www.revenue.wi.gov/forms/excise/index-f.html
Tax deducted from refund:	Yes.
Tax paid on separate return:	No.
Difficulty:	Difficult.
File by:	1 year from the date the fuel was purchased.
Attach documents to claim:	*Fuel Purchase Schedule* listed on page 3 of refund claim (submit instead of invoices) or Invoices.
Send to address:	Wisconsin Department of Revenue Mail Stop 5-107 P.O. Box 8900 Madison, WI 53708
Don't file if:	Claim is for less than 100 gallons or if sales tax is greater than refund. Refunds may not be claimed on fuel purchased for use in the following vehicles: • Snowmobiles. • Recreational motorboats. • All-terrain vehicles unless registered for private use. • Planes.
State statute(s) supporting refund:	§ 78.75(1m).
Keep records on file:	4 years.

<u>Wisconsin Fuel Tax Refund Claim Instructions</u>: Fuel tax refund for gasoline sold by gasoline retailers.

INSTRUCTIONS	
State the fuel is purchased in:	WI
Fuel type:	Gasoline.
Refund type:	Any person who operates a retail service station may claim a refund of one-half of one percent of the Wisconsin motor vehicle fuel tax paid on gasoline received into that person's retail storage facilities.
Form name:	*Retailer's Claim for Gasoline Tax Refund.*
Form #:	**MF-004**.
Obtain required forms from:	http://www.revenue.wi.gov/forms/excise/index-f.html
Tax deducted from refund:	No.
Tax paid on separate return:	No.
Difficulty:	Moderate.
File by:	1 year from the date the fuel was purchased.
Attach documents to claim:	*Fuel Purchase Schedule* listed on page 2 of refund claim (submit instead of invoices) or Invoices
Send to address:	Wisconsin Department of Revenue Mail Stop 5-107 P.O. Box 8900 Madison, WI 53708
Don't file if:	Refunds may not be claimed on the following fuel purchases: • Diesel fuel. • Gasoline purchased by you and resold and shipped to customers without being placed in your retail storage facilities. • Consignment purchases.
State statute(s) supporting refund:	§ 78.20.
Keep records on file:	4 years.

<u>Wisconsin Fuel Tax Refund Claim Instructions</u>: Fuel tax refund for purchasers of aviation fuel in excess of one million gallons during a calendar month.

INSTRUCTIONS	
State the fuel is purchased in:	WI
Fuel type:	Aviation fuel.
Refund type:	This form may be filed by anyone who purchases general aviation fuel in Wisconsin from suppliers in excess of one million gallons during a calendar month. The allowance may not be claimed if you purchase general aviation fuel for resale. The allowance is paid from the petroleum inspection fees collected by the department.
Form name:	*Claim for General Aviation Petroleum Inspection Fee Refund.*
Form #:	**MF-015.**
Obtain required forms from:	http://www.revenue.wi.gov/forms/excise/index-f.html
Tax deducted from refund:	No.
Tax paid on separate return:	No.
Difficulty:	Moderate.
File by:	1 year from the date the fuel was purchased.
Attach documents to claim:	Copies of fuel invoices.
Send to address:	Wisconsin Department of Revenue Mail Stop 5-107 P.O. Box 8900 Madison, WI 53708
Don't file if:	Gallons are less than one million purchased in Wisconsin during a calendar month
State statute(s) supporting refund:	§ 78.75(1m).
Keep records on file:	4 years.

<u>Wisconsin Fuel Tax Refund Claim Instructions</u>: Fuel tax refund for suppliers of fuel for an exempt purpose.

INSTRUCTIONS	
State the fuel is purchased in:	WI
Fuel type:	Gasoline and undyed diesel fuel.
Refund type:	Persons who sell gasoline and/or undyed diesel fuel for exempt use receive a refund of the Wisconsin motor vehicle fuel tax they pay suppliers when purchasing the fuel for resale.
Form name:	*Vendor's Claim for Motor Vehicle Fuel Tax Refund.*
Form #:	**MF-012**.
Obtain required forms from:	http://www.revenue.wi.gov/forms/excise/index-f.html
Tax deducted from refund:	No.
Tax paid on separate return:	No.
Difficulty:	Moderate.
File by:	1 year from the date the fuel was purchased.
Attach documents to claim:	Persons making exempt sales must maintain records of each sale, including the name and address of the buyer, date of sale, the number of gallons sold, type of fuel sold, and the amount of state motor vehicle fuel tax and petroleum inspection fee (when applicable) deducted from the sales price.
Send to address:	Wisconsin Department of Revenue Mail Stop 5-107 P.O. Box 8900 Madison, WI 53708
Don't file if:	Claim is for less than 100 gallons or if sales tax is greater than refund.
State statute(s) supporting refund:	§ 78.01.
Keep records on file:	4 years.

Wisconsin Fuel Tax Refund Claim Instructions: Fuel tax refund for distributors of fuel who sell to another distributor or dealer for resale.

INSTRUCTIONS	
State the fuel is purchased in:	WI
Fuel type:	Gasoline and undyed diesel fuel.
Refund type:	Wisconsin law allows a refund to wholesaler distributors who: • sell motor vehicle fuel (gasoline, undyed diesel) to another wholesaler distributor or retail dealer for resale, and • are not able to recover the Wisconsin motor vehicle fuel tax from that customer. The wholesale distributor is not liable for the uncollectible tax and may apply to the department for a refund of that tax.
Form name:	Wholesaler Distribution Claim for Tax Refund Uncollectible Wisconsin Motor Vehicle Fuel Taxes.
Form #:	**MF-016.**
Obtain required forms from:	http://www.revenue.wi.gov/forms/excise/index-f.html
Tax deducted from refund:	No.
Tax paid on separate return:	No.
Difficulty:	Moderate.
File by:	Within 4 years of the 15th day of the 4th month following the close of your calendar or fiscal year in which the account became worthless.
Attach documents to claim:	List motor vehicle fuel sales on which Wisconsin fuel taxes are uncollectible. Failure to provide all the information may delay the processing of your refund claim.
Send to address:	Wisconsin Department of Revenue Mail Stop 5-107 P.O. Box 8900 Madison, WI 53708
Don't file if:	Fuel tax has not been written off as uncollectible before filing a refund claim.
State statute(s) supporting refund:	§ 4.12.
Keep records on file:	4 years.

WYOMING

Wyoming Fuel Tax Refund Claim Instructions: Fuel tax refund for fuel purchased for farming.

INSTRUCTIONS	
State the fuel is purchased in:	WY
Fuel type:	Excise tax from biodiesel, gasoline and undyed diesel fuel.
Refund type:	Farming equipment.
Form name:	*Agricultural Bulk Gasoline and Undyed Diesel / Biodiesel Tax Refund Request.*
Form #:	**Ag_refund (201111)**
Obtain required forms from:	http://www.dot.state.wy.us/wydot/business_with_wydot/fuel_tax/off_road_refund
Tax deducted from refund:	No, only if copy of sales tax license is provided with refund claim.
Tax paid on separate return:	No.
Difficulty:	Moderate.
File by:	1 year from the date the fuel was purchased.
Attach documents to claim:	Receipts, invoices, or bulk-purchase printouts from the distributor. In-house logs or computer printouts are not permissible as backup.
Send to address:	Department of Transportation Fuel Tax Administration 5300 Bishop Boulevard Cheyenne, WY 82009
Don't file if:	Refund is less than $10.00 annually. Refunds of less than $250.00 per month will be filed quarterly. Refund requests of less than $10.00 will be processed only once in each calendar year.
State statute(s) supporting refund:	§ 39-17-109, 39-17-209.
Keep records on file:	3 years.

Wyoming Fuel Tax Refund Claim Instructions: Fuel tax refund for fuel purchased for school-owned vehicles.

INSTRUCTIONS	
State the fuel is purchased in:	WY
Fuel type:	Gasoline, gasohol, undyed diesel and undyed biodiesel.
Refund type:	Schools, colleges and universities. Other: The University of Wyoming, a community college, or public schools located in Wyoming.
Form name:	*School Districts, Community colleges, and University of Wyoming Gasoline, Gasohol, Undyed Diesel and Undyed Biodiesel Tax Refund Request.*
Form #:	**School_refund (200906)**
Obtain required forms from:	http://www.dot.state.wy.us/wydot/business_with_wydot/fuel_tax/off_road_refund
Tax deducted from refund:	No, only if copy of sales tax license is provided with refund claim.
Tax paid on separate return:	No.
Difficulty:	Moderate.
File by:	1 year from the date the fuel was purchased.
Attach documents to claim:	Documents must be receipts or invoices; in-house logs or computer printouts will be disallowed; card lock or key lock printouts from the vendor are acceptable.
Send to address:	Department of Transportation Fuel Tax Administration 5300 Bishop Boulevard Cheyenne, WY 82009
Don't file if:	Refund is less than $10.00 annually. Refunds of less than $250.00 per month will be filed quarterly. Refund requests of less than $10.00 will be processed only once in each calendar year.
State statute(s) supporting refund:	§ 39-17-109, 39-17-209.
Keep records on file:	3 years.

Wyoming Fuel Tax Refund Claim Instructions: Fuel tax refund for fuel purchased for construction equipment, heating, logging, mining, manufacturing, PTO vehicles, processing, trains and well drilling.

INSTRUCTIONS	
State the fuel is purchased in:	WY
Fuel type:	Undyed diesel and undyed biodiesel.
Refund type:	Construction equipment, heating, logging, mining, manufacturing, PTO (power take-off) vehicles, processing, trains and well drilling.
Form name:	*Undyed Diesel and Undyed Biodiesel Fuel Tax Refund Request*
Form #:	**Equipment Refund (200906).**
Obtain required forms from:	http://www.dot.state.wy.us/wydot/business_with_wydot/fuel_tax/off_road_refund
Tax deducted from refund:	No, only if copy of sales tax license is provided with refund claim.
Tax paid on separate return:	No.
Difficulty:	Moderate.
File by:	1 year from the date the fuel was purchased.
Attach documents to claim:	Documents must be receipts or invoices; in-house logs or computer printouts will be disallowed; card lock or key lock printouts from the Vendor are acceptable.
Send to address:	Department of Transportation Fuel Tax Administration 5300 Bishop Boulevard Cheyenne, WY 82009
Don't file if:	Refund is less than $10.00 annually. Refunds of less than $250.00 per month will be filed quarterly. Refund requests of less than $10.00 will be processed only once in each calendar year.
State statute(s) supporting refund:	§ 39-17-209.
Keep records on file:	3 years.

Wyoming Fuel Tax Refund Claim Instructions: Fuel tax refund for diesel fuel purchased for reefer trailers.

INSTRUCTIONS	
State the fuel is purchased in:	WY
Fuel type:	Undyed diesel fuel.
Refund type:	Refrigeration (reefer) trailers.
Form name:	*Reefer fuel Tax Refund Request Undyed Diesel Fuel Only.*
Form #:	**Reefer Tax Refund (200906).**
Obtain required forms from:	http://www.dot.state.wy.us/wydot/business_with_wydot/fuel_tax/off_road_refund
Tax deducted from refund:	No, only if copy of sales tax license is provided with refund claim.
Tax paid on separate return:	No.
Difficulty:	Moderate.
File by:	1 year from the date the fuel was purchased.
Attach documents to claim:	Documents must be receipts, invoices, or bulk-purchase printouts from the distributor; in-house logs or computer printouts disallowed. Receipts must be sorted by county. All refund requests must be submitted with receipts totaled with an adding machine tape attached to multiple receipts showing the total gallons purchased by county. Enter grand total of all counties as the number of gallons claimed.
Send to address:	Department of Transportation Fuel Tax Administration 5300 Bishop Boulevard Cheyenne, WY 82009
Don't file if:	Refund is less than $10.00 annually. Refunds of less than $250.00 per month will be filed quarterly. Refund requests of less than $10.00 will be processed only once in each calendar year.
State statute(s) supporting refund:	§ 39-17-209.
Keep records on file:	3 years.

<u>Wyoming Fuel Tax Refund Claim Instructions</u>: Fuel tax refund for diesel fuel purchased for non-IFTA vehicles driven off-road in Wyoming.

INSTRUCTIONS	
State the fuel is purchased in:	WY
Fuel type:	Undyed diesel fuel.
Refund type:	Non-IFTA licensed vehicles driven off road in Wyoming using undyed diesel fuel.
Form name:	*"Taxable Fuel/Non-Taxable Fuel" Refund Request* (For "non-IFTA" licensed vehicles driven off road in Wyoming using undyed diesel fuel).
Form #:	**Taxable/Non-Taxable Refund (200906).**
Obtain required forms from:	http://www.dot.state.wy.us/wydot/business_with_wydot/fuel_tax/off_road_refund
Tax deducted from refund:	No, only if copy of sales tax license is provided with refund claim.
Tax paid on separate return:	No.
Difficulty:	Moderate.
File by:	1 year from the date the fuel was purchased.
Attach documents to claim:	Documents must be receipts or invoices; in-house computer printouts disallowed; card lock or key lock printouts from the vendor are acceptable.
Send to address:	Department of Transportation Fuel Tax Administration 5300 Bishop Boulevard Cheyenne, WY 82009
Don't file if:	Refund is less than $10.00 annually. Refunds of less than $250.00 per month will be filed quarterly. Refund requests of less than $10.00 will be processed only once in each calendar year.
State statute(s) supporting refund:	§ 39-17-209.
Keep records on file:	3 years.

Wyoming Fuel Tax Refund Claim Instructions: Fuel tax refund for fuel exports, transfers in inventory, diversions, excess tax collection and bad debt.

INSTRUCTIONS	
State the fuel is purchased in:	WY
Fuel type:	Aviation gasoline, gasoline, gasohol, undyed kerosene, jet fuel and undyed diesel.
Refund type:	Exports, transfers in inventory, diversions, excess tax collection, bad debt.
Form name:	*Wyoming Distributor, Importer, Exporter Monthly Tax Return.*
Form #:	**DIE (201107).**
Obtain required forms from:	http://www.dot.state.wy.us/wydot/business_with_wydot/fuel_tax/off_road_refund
Tax deducted from refund:	No, only if copy of sales tax license is provided with refund claim.
Tax paid on separate return:	No.
Difficulty:	Moderate.
File by:	1 year from the date the fuel was purchased.
Attach documents to claim:	None.
Send to address:	Department of Transportation Fuel Tax Administration 5300 Bishop Boulevard Cheyenne, WY 82009
Don't file if:	You are not a fuel distributor, importer, or exporter.
State statute(s) supporting refund:	§ 39-17-109, 39-17-209.
Keep records on file:	3 years.

Phone Numbers and Addresses

State	Mailing Address	Phone and Fax Numbers
AL	Alabama Department of Revenue Sales, Use & Business Tax Division Motor Fuels Section P.O. Box 327540 Montgomery, AL 36132	Phone: (334) 242-9630 Fax: (334) 242-9662
AK	Alaska Department of Revenue Tax Division P.O. Box 110420 Juneau, AK 99811	Phone: (907) 269-6948 Fax: (907) 465-2375
AZ	Arizona Department of Transportation Fuel Tax Refund Compliance Unit Mail Drop 521M P.O. Box 2100 Phoenix AZ 85001	Phone: (602) 712-8727
AR	Arkansas Department of Revenue Motor Fuel Tax Section P.O. Box 1752 Little Rock, AR 72203	Phone: (501) 682-4800 Fax: (501) 682-5599
CA	California State Board of Equalization Motor Carrier Section 450 N. St. MIC 65 P.O. Box 942879 Sacramento, CA 94279	Phone: (916) 22-9669 Toll-Free Phone: (800) 400-7115 Fax: (916) 323-4404 Additional Fax: (916) 323-9352

State	Mailing Address	Phone and Fax Numbers
CO	Colorado Department of Revenue Taxpayer Service Division Special Tax Section 1375 Sherman St., Rm. 200 Denver, CO 80261	Phone: (303) 205-8205
CT	Connecticut Department of Revenue Services State of Connecticut Excise Taxes Unit 25 Sigourney St., Ste. 2 Hartford CT 06106	Phone: (860) 541-3224 Phone (Outside CT): (860) 297-5962 Toll-Free Phone: (800) 382-9463 (Within CT-Outside Greater Hartford area only) TDD/TT Users only: (860) 297-4911
DE	State of Delaware Motor Fuel Tax Administration P.O. Drawer E. Dover, DE 19903	Phone: (302) 744-2724
DC	Washington, D.C. Office of Tax and Revenue P.O. Box 556 Washington, DC 20044	Phone: (202) 442-6313
FL	Florida Department of Revenue Refunds Subprocess P.O. Box 6490 Tallahassee FL 32314	Phone: (850) 617-8585 Fax: (850) 410-2526
GA	Georgia Department of Revenue Motor Fuel Tax Unit Refund Section 1800 Century Center Blvd. NE.,Ste. 8223 Atlanta, GA 30345	Phone: (404) 417-6712 Fax: (404) 968-0778
HI	State of Hawaii Department of Taxation P.O. Box 259 Honolulu, HI 96809	Phone: (808) 587-1791 Fax: (808) 587-1560
ID	Idaho State Tax Commission P.O. Box 76 Boise ID 83707	Phone: (208) 334-7660 Toll-Free Phone: (800) 972-7660
IL	Motor Fuel Tax Refund Illinois Department of Revenue P.O. Box 19019 Springfield, IL 62794	Phone: (217) 782-3336 Toll-Free Phone: (800) 732-8866
IN	Indiana Department of Revenue P.O. Box 6080 Indianapolis, IN 46206	Phone: (317) 615-2720 Phone: (317) 615-2559

State	Mailing Address	Phone and Fax Numbers
IA	Iowa Dept. of Revenue Motor Fuel Unit Examination Section P.O. Box 10456 Des Moines, IA 50306	Phone (Iowa, Omaha, Rock Island, Moline): (800) 367-3388 Phone (local, out of state): (515) 281-3114 Fax: (515) 281-3756
KS	Kansas Department of Revenue Docking State Office Bldg., Motor Fuel 915 SW. Harrison St. Topeka, KS 66625	Phone: (785) 296-7048 Phone: (785) 296-5327 Fax: (785) 296-4993
KY	Kentucky Department of Revenue Motor Fuels Tax Section Station 63 P.O. Box 1303 Frankfort, KY 40602	Phone: (502) 564-3853
LA	Louisiana Department of Revenue Taxpayer Services Division Excise Taxes Section P. O. Box 201 Baton Rouge, LA 70821	Phone: (225) 219-7656 Phone (TDD): (225) 219-2114
ME	Maine Revenue Service P.O. Box 1065 Augusta, ME 04332	Phone: (207) 624-9609 Fax: (207) 287-6628
MI	Michigan Department of Treasury P.O. Box 30474 Lansing, MI 48909	Phone: (517) 636-4600 Fax: (517) 636-4593
MN	Minnesota Revenue Petroleum Taxes Mail Station 3333 St. Paul, MN 55146	Phone: (651) 296-0889 (TTY: Call 711 for Minnesota Relay)
MS	Mississippi Department of Revenue P. O. Box 1033 Jackson, MS 39215	Phone: (601) 923-7150
MA	Massachusetts Department of Revenue P.O. Box 7012 Boston, MA 02204	Phone: (617) 887-MDOR Toll-Free Phone: (800) 392-6089
MD	Comptroller of Maryland Revenue Administration Division Revenue Administration Center Annapolis, MD 21411	Phone: (410) 260-7131 Fax: (410) 974-2243

State	Mailing Address	Phone and Fax Numbers
MO	Missouri Department of Revenue Taxation Division P.O. Box 800 Jefferson City, MO 65105	Phone: (573) 751-7671 Phone (TDD): (800) 735-2966
MT	Montana Department of Transportation 2701 Prospect Ave. P.O. Box 201001 Helena MT 59620	Phone: (406) 444-7278 Phone (TTY): (800) 335-7592 Fax: (406) 444-7276
NC	North Carolina Department of Revenue Excise Tax Division P.O. Box 25000 Raleigh, North Carolina 27640	Phone: (919) 733-3409 Toll-Free Phone: (877) 308-9092
ND	Office of North Dakota State Tax Commissioner 600 E. Boulevard Ave., Dept. 127 Bismarck, ND 58505	Phone: (701) 328-7088 Fax: (701) 328-3700 Toll-Free Phone: (877) 328-7088
NE	Motor Fuels Division Nebraska Department of Revenue P.O. Box 98904 Lincoln, NE 68509	Phone: (800) 554-3835 Phone: (402) 471-5730 Fax: (402) 471-5607
NV	Nevada Department of Motor Vehicles Motor Carrier Division 555 Wright Wy. Carson City, NV 89711	Phone (Reno/Sparks/Carson City): (775) 684-4711 Phone (Las Vegas): (702) 486-4368 Ext 5 Rural Nevada (Toll Free): (877) 368-7828 Ext 5 Fax (775) 684-4619
NH	State of New Hampshire Department of Safety Road Toll Bureau 33 Hazen Dr. Concord, NH 03305	Phone: (603) 271-2302 Phone (TDD): 1-800-735-2964
NJ	New Jersey Division of Taxation Motor Fuels Group, Office Audit 50 Barrack St. Trenton, New Jersey 08646	Phone: (609) 292-6400
NM	Revenue Processing Division - Special Tax Programs & Services P.O. Box 25123 Santa Fe, NM 87504	Phone: (505) 827-0800 Phone: (505) 827-0764

State	Mailing Address	Phone and Fax Numbers
NY	NYS Tax Department Fuel Tax Refund Unit P.O. Box 5501 Albany, NY 12205	Phone: (518) 457-5735
OH	Ohio Department of Taxation Motor Fuel Refund Unit P.O. Box 530 Columbus, OH 43216	Phone: (855) 466-3921 Fax: (614) 752-864
OK	Oklahoma Tax Commission Account Maintenance Division Credits and Refunds Section 2501 Lincoln Blvd. Oklahoma City, OK 73194	Phone: (405) 521-3683
OR	ODOT Fuels Tax Group 550 Capitol St. N. Salem, OR 97301	Phone: (503) 378-8150 Fax: (503) 378-3060
PA	Pennsylvania Bureau of Motor Fuel Taxes P.O. Box 280646 Harrisburg, PA 17128	Phone: (717) 783-9367 Fax: (717) 787-6261
RI	Rhode Island Division of Taxation One Capitol Hill Providence, RI 02908	Phone: (401) 574-8955
SC	South Carolina Department of Revenue Motor Fuel Columbia, SC 29214	Phone: (803) 896-1990
SD	South Dakota Department of Revenue 445 East Capitol Ave. Pierre, SD 57501	Phone: (605)-773-3541 Fax: (605)-773-2550
TN	Tennessee Department of Revenue Andrew Jackson Bldg. 500 Deaderick St. Nashville, TN 37242	Phone: (615) 253-0600
TX	Texas Comptroller of Public Accounts 111 E. 17th St. Austin, TX 78774	Toll-Free Phone: (800) 252-1383 Phone: (512) 463-4600 Fax: (512) 475-5424
UT	Utah State Tax Commission 210 N. 1950 W. Salt Lake City, UT 84134	Phone: (801) 297-2200 Phone (Outside the Salt Lake area): (800) 662-4335

State	Mailing Address	Phone and Fax Numbers
VA	Department of Motor Vehicles Tax Services Refund Section P. O. Box 27422 Richmond, VA 23261	Phone: (804) 497-7100 Phone (TTY): (800) 272-9268 Fax: (804) 378-3444
VT	Vermont Commercial Vehicle Operations 120 State St. Montpelier, VT 05603	Phone: (802) 828-2000 Phone: (802) 828-2070 Phone: (802) 828-5787
WA	Washington Department of Revenue Fuel Tax Refund Unit Dept. of Licensing P.O. Box 9228 Olympia, WA 98507	Phone: (360) 664-1838 Fax: (360) 570-7843
WV	State of West Virginia State Tax Department Tax Account Administration Division P.O. Box 2991 Charleston, WV 25330	Phone: (304) 558-3333 Toll-Free Phone: (800) 982-829
WI	Wisconsin Department of Revenue Excise Tax Section 6-107 P.O. Box 8900 Madison WI 53708	Phone: (608) 266-0064 Fax: (606) 261-7049
WY	Wyoming Department of Transportation Fuel Tax Administration 5300 Bishop Blvd. Cheyenne, WY 82009	Phone: (307) 777- 3947 Phone: (307) 777- 4856 Fax: (307) 777- 4769

About the author

Justin Dougherty is an Arizona native who has more than 12 years of tax experience in the transportation, fuel recycling, shipping and airline industries. ***The Ultimate Fuel Tax Refund Guide*** is his first book.

In 2001 he graduated from the W.P. Carey School of Business at Arizona State University with a Bachelor's Degree in Computer Information Systems. He is the CEO of Fleetmasters, a fleet compliance company in Peoria, Arizona.

Justin is married and lives in Phoenix with his wife.

www.ingramcontent.com/pod-product-compliance
Lightning Source LLC
LaVergne TN
LVHW051127210926
848482LV00001B/10